ENGLISH TRAGEDY, 1370-1600:
FIFTY YEARS OF CRITICISM

ENGLISH TRAGEDY, 1370-1600: FIFTY YEARS OF CRITICISM

Compiled by
Harry B. Caldwell
and
David L. Middleton

TRINITY UNIVERSITY PRESS • SAN ANTONIO, TEXAS

Checklists in the Humanities
and Education: a Series

As a continuing effort, *Checklists in the Humanities and Education: A Series* endeavors to provide the student with essential bibliographical information, on important scholarly subjects, not readily available in composite form. The series emphasizes selection and limitation of both primary and secondary works, providing a practical and convenient research tool as a primary aim. For example, this present compilation of criticism devoted to English tragedy, c. 1370-1600, generally omits scholarship which deals with the cultural, philosophical, or historical context out of which the literary forms developed. It treats the primary material as outlined in the Preface below. Likewise, subsequent volumes, which derive from the areas represented by the editorial committee of the series, will remain characteristically selective, limited, and concise. The compilers anticipate that the checklists will help primarily the undergraduate who is often somewhat dismayed by the weight of research materials used by graduate students and faculty.

———————●●●———————

Editorial Committee

Harry B. Caldwell, General Coordinator

Ernest Bufkin, English Literature, University of Georgia
Annelise Duncan, German, Trinity University

M. Thomas Inge, American Literature, Virginia Commonwealth
    University
Lamire Moore, Education, University of Arkansas
William Parrish, History, Westminster College (Mo.)
Frederick J. Streng, Religion, Southern Methodist University
Vern G. Williamsen, Spanish, University of Missouri—Columbia

PREFACE

English Tragedy, 1370-1600: Fifty Years of Criticism lists English tragical literature defined by thematic and formal criteria. Primary works cited in this checklist are of two types:

1. Verse non-dramatic (*De casibus*) tragedy, including Chaucer's *Troilus and Criseyde* and the *Mirror* tradition, the former owing to the poet's own definition and to general critical consensus. Thus, Henryson's *Testament of Cresseid* is logically included; but Malory, conversely, has been excluded, since, despite the obvious tragic implications in the *Morte d'Arthur,* he writes in prose. Moreover, Malory's Arthurian narrative is most profitably studied within the context of romance. The tragic ballad has been omitted from Section III of this checklist for reasons of length.

2. Dramatic tragedy exclusive of Marlowe and Shakespeare. In some instances, where it seems justified on the basis of Willard Farnham's excellent analysis (see # 699), certain medieval morality plays that show a formal relation to tragedy have been included.

With regard to both primary and secondary works, we have emphasized workability as our primary intention, subordinating attention to exhaustive details of compilation.[1]

---

[1]It is our desire to contribute to the research tools already available in this area: for example, the relevant portions of the standard bibliographies of Miss E. P. Hammond, D. D. Griffith, W. R. Crawford, A. C. Baugh, S. A. Tannenbaum, F. P. Wilson, C. A. Pennel, or Carl J. Stratman's *Bibliography of English Printed Tragedy: 1565-1900.*

Secondary materials cited are mainly scholarly articles which have appeared from 1919 to 1969. Wherever 1970 bibliographers were available, however, we have made use of them in order to bring this compilation as nearly up-to-date as possible. Also included are book-length studies and dissertations specifically devoted to the subject of tragedy or to one of the primary works. On the other hand, broad studies (such as critical biographies) have been limited essentially to those published in the last ten years. Furthermore, in the citation of such general studies, reference is made to the specific passages a reader is likely to find pertinent to a given primary work. Readily available and standard editions are indicated by asterisk.

The checklist has two major divisions, one minor division, and an appendix. The non-dramatic and dramatic tragedies referred to above comprise the major sections, within which primary works are listed for the most part chronologically. Criticism of individual works is then cited alphabetically.[2] The minor section (III) lists general and miscellaneous studies, including selected primary works peripheral to the material of Sections I, II. The appendix lists primary works which have received virtually no critical treatment. We hope that here the enterprising student will find an outlet for his energies. Wherever possible, studies cited have been examined personally, to check both the accuracy of the entry and the relevance of the study to the general topic at hand.

We wish to thank Professors Edgar H. Duncan of Vanderbilt University, and George L. Geckle of the University of South Carolina for their helpful reading of the manuscript and for their pertinent suggestions; the staffs of the Trinity University Libraries and the University of Texas Libraries in Austin; the Faculty Research and Development Committee of Trinity University for a grant to help defray costs of preparing the checklist; and Mrs. Mary McCullough and Mr. William Bondurant, graduate students at Trinity University, for their tireless work in many aspects of manuscript preparation.

HBC
DLM
San Antonio, Texas
December 1970

[2]In their form, entries follow the latest *PMLA* system. Thus: 350. Cauthen, I. B., Jr. *"Gorboduc, Ferrex and Porrex:* the First Two Quartos," *SB,* 15 (1962): 231-233, is item # 350 in the bibliography. The author is I. B. Cauthen, Jr., his article *"Gorboduc, Ferrex and Porrex:* the First Two Quartos." It appeared in *Studies in Bibliography* (see the list of abbreviations), volume 15, in 1962, and is found on pages 231-233.

Contents

ABBREVIATIONS[1]

AL	American Literature
AmRev	American Review
AN&Q	American Notes and Queries
AnM	Annuale Mediaevale
Archiv	Archiv für das Studium der Neueren Sprachen und Literaturen
ArlQ	Arlington Quarterly
BB	Bulletin of Bibliography
BFLS	Bulletin de la Faculté des Lettres de Strasbourg
BHR	Bibliothèque d'Humanisme et Renaissance
BJRL	Bulletin of the John Rylands Library
BPLQ	Boston Public Library Quarterly
BRMMLA	Bulletin of the Rocky Mountain Modern Language Association
BSUF	Ball State University Forum
Bull. Hist. Med.	Bulletin of the History of Medicine
BUSE	Boston University Studies in English
C&M	Classica et Mediaevalia (Copenhagen)
CE	College English

[1]See also the list of abbreviations and short titles in the *PMLA* and Modern Humanities Research Association annual bibliographies.

ChauR	The Chaucer Review
CJ	Classical Journal
CL	Comparative Literature
CLAJ	College Language Association Journal
CQ	The Cambridge Quarterly
CR	The Critical Review (Melbourne, Sidney)
DA	Dissertation Abstracts
DelN	Delaware Notes
DL	Deutsche Literaturzeitung (Berlin)
DM	The Dublin Magazine (formerly The Dubliner)
DramS	Drama Survey
DR	Dalhousie Review
DSPS	Duquesne Studies, Philology Series
DUJ	Durham University Journal
EA	Etudes Anglaises
E&S	Essays and Studies by Members of the English Association
EC	Etudes Celtiques
EETS	Early English Text Society
EIC	Essays in Criticism
ELH	Journal of English Literary History
ELN	English Language Notes
EM	English Miscellany
ER	Etudes Rabelaisiennes
ES	English Studies
ESA	English Studies in Africa (Johannesburg)
EStudien	Englische Studien
Expl	Explicator
FP	Filoloski Pregled (Belgrade)
God.	Godisnik na Sofijskija Universitet, Istoriko-filologiciski Fakultet (Annuaire de l'universite de Sofia, faculte historico-philologique)
HAB	Humanities Association Bulletin (Canada)
HLQ	Huntington Library Quarterly
ISLL	Illinois Studies in Language and Literature
JBS	Journal of British Studies
JEGP	Journal of English and Germanic Philology
JDSG	Jahrbuch der Deutschen Schiller-Gesellschaft
JHI	Journal of the History of Ideas
JWCI	Journal of the Warburg and Courtauld Institute
KN	Kwartalnik Neofilologiczny (Warsaw)
L&P	Literature and Psychology
LanM	Les Langues Modernes
LangQ	Language Quarterly
LHB	Loch Haven Bulletin

LSE	Lund Studies in English
LSUSHS	Louisiana State University Studies, Humanities Series
MAE	Medium Aevum
MLN	Modern Language Notes
MLQ	Modern Language Quarterly
MLR	Modern Language Review
MP	Modern Philology
MR	Massachusetts Review
MS	Mediaeval Studies
N&Q	Notes and Queries
NM	Neuphilologische Mitteilungen
OL	Orbis Litterarum
PAPS	Proceedings of the American Philosophical Society
PBA	Proceedings of the British Academy
PBSA	Papers of the Bibliographical Society of America
PELL	Papers on Language and Literature
PMLA	Publications of the Modern Language Association of America
PMASAL	Papers of the Michigan Academy of Science, Arts, and Letters
PQ	Philological Quarterly
PsyR	Psychoanalytic Review
QR	Quarterly Review
REL	Review of English Literature
RES	Review of English Studies
RenD	Renaissance Drama
RenP	Renaissance Papers
RenQ	Renaissance Quarterly
RevAnglo-Amer	Revue Anglo-Américaine
RIP	Rice Institute Pamphlets
RLC	Revue de Littérature Comparée
RLV	Revue des Langues Vivantes (Bruxelles)
RMS	Renaissance and Modern Studies (Nottingham)
RN	Renaissance News
RORD	Research Opportunities in Renaissance Drama
RS	Research Studies (Washington State University)
RR	Romanic Review
RRDS	Regents Renaissance Drama Series
SAB	South Atlantic Bulletin
SAQ	South Atlantic Quarterly
SB	Studies in Bibliography: Papers of the Bibliographical Society of the University of Virginia
SBoc	Studi sul Boccaccio
SEL	Studies in English Literature, 1500-1900
SELit	Studies in English Literature (English Literary Society of Japan, University of Tokyo)

SFQ	Southern Folklore Quarterly
ShN	Shakespeare Newsletter
ShS	Shakespeare Survey
ShStud	Shakespeare Studies (Tokyo)
ShJB	Shakespeare Jahrbuch
SN	Studia Neophilologica
SP	Studies in Philology
Spec	Speculum
SQ	Shakespeare Quarterly
SR	Sewanee Review
SRen	Studies in the Renaissance
SSL	Studies in Scottish Literature
SSF	Studies in Short Fiction
TCV	Twentieth Century Views
TEAS	Twayne English Authors Series
TLS	(London) Times Literary Supplement
TN	Theatre Notebook
TSE	Tulane Studies in English
TSL	Tennessee Studies in Literature
TSLL	Texas Studies in Language and Literature
UES	Unisa English Studies
UTQ	University of Toronto Quarterly
Ventures	Yale Graduate School Magazine
WHR	Western Humanities Review
YR	Yale Review
YSE	Yale Studies in English

I. NON-DRAMATIC TRAGEDY: THE *DE CASIBUS* TRADITION

I. NON-DRAMATIC TRAGEDY:
THE *DE CASIBUS* TRADITION

GEOFFREY CHAUCER

Monkes Tale (c. 1370-1380)

1. Aiken, P. "Vincent of Beauvais and Chaucer's *Monk's Tale*," *Spec,* 17 (1942): 56-68.

2. Ayres, H. M. "Chaucer and Seneca," *RR,* 10 (1919): 1-15.

3. Babcock, R. W. "The Mediaeval Setting of Chaucer's *Monk's Tale*," *PMLA,* 46 (1931): 205-213.

4. Bassan, M. "Chaucer's 'Cursed Monk,' Constantinus Africanus," *MS,* 24 (1962): 127-140.

5. Beichner, P. E. "Daun Piers, Monk and Business Administrator," *Spec,* 34 (1959): 611-619.

6. Bennett, H. S. "Medieval Literature and the Modern Reader," *E&S,* 31 (1945): 7-18.

7. Braddy, H. "Chaucer's Don Pedro and the Purpose of the *Monk's Tale*," *MLQ,* 13 (1952): 3-5.

8. Braddy, H. "Two Chaucer Notes: Chaucer on Murder: 'De Petro Rege de Cipro'; Bretheren Two; 'Thilke Wikke Ensample of Canacee'," *MLN,* 62 (1947): 173-179.

9. Braddy, H. "The Two Petros in the *Monkes Tale,"* *PMLA,* 50 (1935): 69-80.

10. Bressie, R. "Chaucer's Monk Again," *MLN,* 56 (1941): 161-162.

11. Bressie, R. " 'A Governour Wily and Wys'," *MLN,* 54 (1939): 477-490.

12. Brewer, D. S. "Brutus' Crime: a Footnote to *Julius Caesar,"* RES, 3 (1952): 51-54.

13. Brown, J. O. "Chaucer's Daun Piers: One Monk or Two?" *Criticism,* 6 (1964): 44-52.

14. Byers, J. R., Jr. "Harry Bailey's St. Madrian," *ELN,* 4 (1966): 6-9.

15. Coulter, C. G. "A Song for Men in Days to Come," *American Journal of Archaeology,* 54 (1950): 193-202.

16. Crawford, S. J. "Chaucer and St. Augustine," *TLS,* November 13, 1930, p. 942.

17. Crawford, S. J. "Croesus's Dream," *TLS,* June 26, 1924, p. 404.

18. Dedeck-Héry, V. "Le Boèce de Chaucer et les manuscrits français de la Consolatio de J. de Meun," *PMLA,* 59 (1944): 18-25.

19. Delasanta, R. K. " 'Namoore of this': Chaucer's Priest and Monk," *TSL,* 13 (1968): 117-132.

20. Donovan, M. J. "Three Notes on Chaucerian Marine Life," *PQ,* 31 (1952): 439-441.

21. Dwyer, R. A. "Some Readers of John Trevisa," *N&Q,* 14 (1967): 291-292.

22. Forster, M. "Boccaccio's *De casibus vivorum illustrium* in Englischen Bearbeitung," *DL,* 45 (1924): 1943-46.

23. Frank, G. "Chaucer's Monk," *MLN,* 55 (1940): 780-781.

24. Frost, G. L. " 'That Precious Corpus Madrian'," *MLN,* 57 (1942): 177-179.

25. Garbáty, T. J. "The Monk and the *Merchant's Tale:* An Aspect of Chaucer's Building Process in the *Canterbury Tales,"* *MP,* 67 (1969): 18-24.

26. Gathercole, P. M. "Illuminations on *Des cas des nobles* (Boccaccio's *De casibus*)," *SBoc,* 2 (1964): 343-356.

27. Gathercole, P. M. "Illuminations on the French Boccaccio Manuscripts," *SBoc,* 1 (1963): 387-414.

28. Gillmeister, H. "Chaucer's Mönch and die 'Reule of Seint Maure or of Seint Beneit'," *NM,* 69 (1968): 222-232.

29. Grennen, J. E. "Chaucer's Monk: Baldness, Venery, and Embonpoint," *AN&Q,* 6 (1968): 83-85.

30. Grennen, J. E. "Chaucerian Portraiture: Medicine and the Monk," *NM,* 69 (1968): 569-574.

31. Grennen, J. E. " 'Sampsoun' in the *Canterbury Tales:* Chaucer Adapting a Source," *NM,* 67 (1966): 117-122.

32. Hall, L. B., ed. Introduction to *De casibus virorum illustrium by Giovanni Boccaccio: a Facsimile Reproduction of the Paris Edition of 1520.* Gainesville, 1962, pp. v-xi (trans. and abridged by L. B. Hall, New York, 1965).

33. Hamilton, M. P. "Bernard the Monk: Postscript," *MLN,* 62 (1947): 190-191.

34. Hammerle, K. "Das Fortunamotiv von Chaucer bis Bacon," *Anglia,* 65 (1941): 87-100.

35. Haskell, A. S. "The Host's 'Precious Corpus Madrian'," *JEGP,* 67 (1968): 430-440.

36. Hoffman, R. L. "Ovid and the Monk's Tale of Hercules," *N&Q,* 12 (1965): 406-409.

37. Johnson, D. R. "The Biblical Characters of Chaucer's Monk," *PMLA,* 66 (1951): 827-843.

38. Jones, C. "The *Monk's Tale,* a Mediaeval Sermon," *MLN,* 52 (1937): 570-572.

39. Kaske, R. E. "The Knight's Interruption of the *Monk's Tale,"* *ELH,* 24 (1957): 249-268.

40. Kuhl, E. P. "Chaucer's Monk," *MLN,* 55 (1940): 480.

41. Luke, H. C. "Visitors from the East to the Plantagenet and Lancastrian Kings," *Nineteenth Century,* 108 (1930): 760-769.

42. McCray, C. L. "Chaucer and Lydgate, and the Uses of History,"
    DA, 29 (1969): 4461A-62A (U. of Nebraska).

43. McDermott, W. C. "Chaucer and Virgil," *C&M,* 23 (1962):
    216-217.

44. Malone, K. "Harry Bailly and Godelief," *ES,* 31 (1950): 209-
    215.

45. Maynard, T. "Chaucer's Monk," *Month,* Feb., 1935, pp. 165-
    168.

46. Moorman, C. "Courtly Love in Chaucer," *ELH,* 27 (1960):
    163-173.

47. Norris, D. M. "Harry Bailey's 'Corpus Madrian'," *MLN,* 48
    (1933): 146-148.

48. Oruch, J. B. "Chaucer's Worldly Monk," *Criticism,* 8 (1966):
    280-288.

49. Pace, G. B. "Adam's Hell," *PMLA,* 78 (1963): 25-35.

50. Patch, H. R. "Chaucer and Lady Fortune," *MLR,* 22 (1927):
    377-388.

51. Patch, H. R. "Necessity in Boethius and the Neoplatonists,"
    Spec, 10 (1935): 393-404.

52. Patch, H. R. "The Tradition of the Goddess Fortuna," *Smith
    College Studies in Modern Languages,* III (1921-1922):
    131-235.

53. Pratt, R. A. "Chaucer and the Pillars of Hercules," in *Studies
    in Honor of Ullman,* ed. by L. B. Lawler, et al. St. Louis,
    1960, pp. 118-125.

54. Prins, A. A. "Two Notes on the Prologue of Chaucer's *Canter-
    bury Tales," ES,* 30 (1949): 42-44, 83-86.

55. Reiss, E. "The Symbolic Surface of the *Canterbury Tales:* The
    Monk's Portrait," *ChauR,* 2 (1968): 254-272; 3 (1968):
    12-28.

56. Richardson, H. G. "Godeleef My Wyf," *TLS,* January 20, 1927,
    p. 44.

57. Rickert, E. "Godeleef My Wyf," *TLS,* December 16, 1926, p.
    935.

58. Rickert, E. "Goode Lief, My Wyf," *MP,* 25 (1927): 79-82.

59. Robbins, R. H. "A New Chaucer Analogue: The Legend of Ugolino," *Trivium,* 2 (1967): 1-15.

60. *Robinson, F. N., ed. Notes to *The Works of Geoffrey Chaucer.* 2nd ed. Boston, 1961, pp. 745-750.

61. Root, R. K. "The *Monk's Tale,*" in *Sources and Analogues of Chaucer's Canterbury Tales,* ed. by W. F. Bryan and G. Dempster. New York, 1958 (Chicago, 1941), pp. 615-644.

62. Savage, H. "Chaucer and the 'Pitous Deeth' of 'Petro, Glorie of Spayne'," *Spec,* 24 (1949): 357-375.

63. Seaton, E. " 'Goode Lief My Wife'," *MLR,* 41 (1946): 196-202.

64. Silverstein, H. T. "Chaucer's 'Brutus Cassius'," *MLN,* 47 (1932): 148-150.

65. Smith, R. M. "Bernard the Monk: Nota Amplificata," *MLN,* 62 (1947): 910-935.

66. Socola, E. M. "Chaucer's Development of Fortune in the *Monk's Tale,*" *JEGP,* 49 (1950): 159-171.

67. Spencer, T. "The Story of Ugolino in Dante and Chaucer," *Spec,* 9 (1934): 295-301 (in *Theodore Spencer: Selected Essays,* 1968, pp. 41-48).

68. Stavrou, C. N. "Some Implications of Chaucer's Irony," *SAQ,* 56 (1957): 454-461.

69. Strange, W. C. "The *Monk's Tale:* A Generous View," *ChauR,* 1 (1967): 167-180.

70. Tatlock, J. S. P. "Chaucer's 'Bernard the Monk'," *MLN,* 46 (1931): 21-23.

71. Tatlock, J. S. P. "Chaucer's Monk," *MLN,* 55 (1940): 350-354.

72. Ussery, H. E. "The Status of Chaucer's Monk: Clerical, Official, Social, and Moral," *TSE,* 17 (1969): 1-30.

73. Visser, F. Th. "This Ilke Monke Leet Olde Thynges Pace," *ES,* 30 (1949): 133.

74. Watson, C. S. "The Relationship of the *Monk's Tale* and the *Nun's Priest's Tale,*" *SSF,* 1 (1964): 277-288.

75. Willard, R. "Chaucer's 'Text That Seith That Hunters Been Nat Hooly Men'," *Studies in English, University of Texas* (1947): 209-251.

76. Wittcutt, W. B. "Chaucer's Boethius," *AmRev,* 8 (1936): 61-70.

77. Young, K. "Chaucer's 'Vitremyte'," *SP,* 40 (1943): 494-501.

See also 147, 164, 182, 185, 196, 198, 689, 697, 699, 712.

Troilus and Criseyde (c. 1382-1386)

78. Adams, J. F. "Irony in Troilus' Apostrophe to the Vacant House of Criseyde," *MLQ,* 24 (1963): 61-65.

79. apRoberts, R. P. "The Central Episode in Chaucer's *Troilus,*" *PMLA,* 77 (1962): 373-385.

80. apRoberts, R. P. "Criseyde and the Moral of Chaucer's *Troilus,*" Berkeley, 1950 (summary of thesis).

81. apRoberts, R. P. "Criseyde's Infidelity and the Moral of the *Troilus,*" *Spec,* 44 (1969): 383-402.

82. Askew, M. W. "Courtly Love: Neurosis as Institution," *PsyR,* 52 (1965): 19-29.

83. Bartel, N. A. "Child of Night," *BSUF,* 6 (1965): 45-50.

84. Baugh, A. C. "Chaucer's *Troilus,* iv. 1585: a Biblical Allusion?" *MLN,* 76 (1961): 1-4.

85. Bayley, J. *The Characters of Love: a Study in the Literature of Personality.* London, 1960, pp. 49-123.

86. Bessent, B. R. "The Puzzling Chronology of Chaucer's *Troilus,*" *SN,* 41 (1969): 99-111.

87. Bloomfield, M. W. "Distance and Predestination in *Troilus and Criseyde,*" *PMLA,* 72 (1957): 14-26.

88. Bloomfield, M. W. "The Eighth Sphere: a Note on Chaucer's *Troilus and Criseyde,* v. 1809," *MLR,* 53 (1958): 408-410.

89. Bolton, W. F. "Treason in *Troilus,*" *Archiv,* 203 (1966): 255-262.

90. Bothwick, Sister M. C. "Antigone's Song as 'Mirour' in Chaucer's *Troilus and Criseyde,*" *MLQ,* 22 (1961): 227-235.

91. Bowers, R. H. "The 'Suttell and Dissayvabull' World of Chaucer's *Troilus,*" *N&Q,* 202 (1957): 278-279.

92. Brenner, G. "Narrative Structure in Chaucer's *Troilus and Criseyde,*" *AnM,* 6 (1965): 5-18.

93. Bullett, G. "The Fortunes of Cressida," *New Statesman*, 21 (1923): 361-363.

94. Clark, J. W. "Dante and the Epilogue of *Troilus*," *JEGP*, 50 (1951): 1-10.

95. Cope, J. I. "Chaucer, Venus and the 'Seventhe Spere'," *MLN*, 67 (1952): 245-246.

96. Corsa, H. S. *Chaucer: Poet of Mirth and Morality*. Notre Dame, 1964, pp. 40-70.

97. Corsa, H. S. "Is This a Mannes Herte?" *L&P*, 16 (1966): 184-191.

98. Costello, Sister M. A. "The Goddes and God in the *Troilus*," *DA*, 23 (1963): 3352 (Fordham).

99. Covella, Sister F. D. "Audience as Determinant of Meaning in *Troilus*," *ChauR*, 2 (1968): 235-245.

100. Craig, H. "From Gorgias to Troilus," in *Studies in Medieval Literature in Honor of Professor Albert Croll Baugh*, ed. by M. Leach. Philadelphia, 1961, pp. 97-107.

101. Curry, W. C. *Chaucer and the Mediaeval Sciences*. Revised and enlarged edition. New York, 1960, pp. 241-298.

102. Curry, W. C. "Destiny in Chaucer's *Troilus*," *PMLA*, 45 (1930): 129-168.

103. Curry, W. C. "Fortuna Maior," *MLN*, 38 (1923): 94-96.

104. Daly, S. R. "Criseyde's Blasphemous Aube," *N&Q*, 10 (1963): 442-444.

105. D'Ardenne, S. R. T. O. *"Troilus and Criseyde* and 'The Tragic Comedians'," *ES*, 44 (1963): 12-19.

106. David, A. "The Hero of the *Troilus*," *Spec*, 37 (1962): 566-581.

107. Denomy, A. "The Two Moralities of Chaucer's *Troilus and Criseyde*," *Trans. Royal Soc. of Canada*, sec. 2, 44 (1950): 35-46.

108. Donaldson, E. T. "Chaucer's *Troilus*, iv. 1585: a Biblical Allusion?" *MLN*, 76 (1961): 4-5.

109. Donaldson, E. T. "The Ending of Chaucer's *Troilus*," in *Early English and Norse Studies, Presented to Hugh Smith . . .*, ed. by A. Brown and P. Foote. London, 1963, pp. 26-45.

110. Donaldson, E. T. "The Myth of Courtly Love," *Ventures,* 6 (1965): 16-23.

111. Dronke, P. "The Conclusion of *Troilus and Criseyde,*" *MAE,* 33 (1964): 47-52.

112. Dunning, T. P. "God and Man in *Troilus and Criseyde,*" in *English and Medieval Studies, Presented* to *J. R. R. Tolkien . . .,* ed. by N. Davis and C. L. Wrenn. London, 1962, pp. 164-182.

113. Durham, L. J. "Love and Death in *Troilus and Criseyde,*" *ChauR,* 3 (1968): 1-11.

114. Elbow, P. "Two Boethian Speeches in *Troilus and Criseyde* and Chaucerian Irony," in *Literary Criticism and Historical Understanding: Selected Papers from the English Institute,* comp. by Phillip Damon. New York, 1967, pp. 85-107.

115. Erzgräber, W. "Tragik und Komik in Chaucer's *Troilus and Criseyde,*" in *Festschrift für Walter Hübner.* Berlin, 1964, pp. 139-163.

116. Evans, L. G. "A Biblical Allusion in *Troilus and Criseyde,*" *MLN,* 74 (1959): 584-587.

117. Everett, D. *"Troilus and Criseyde,"* in *Essays on Middle English Literature,* ed. by P. Kean. London, 1955, chp. 5.

118. Farnham, A. E. "Chaucerian Irony and the Ending of the *Troilus,*" *ChauR,* 1 (1967): 207-216.

119. Farnham, W. *The Medieval Heritage of Elizabethan Tragedy.* Oxford, 1963 (Berkeley, 1936), pp. 137-160.

120. Fowler, D. C. "An Unusual Meaning of 'Win' in Chaucer's *Troilus and Criseyde,*" *MLN,* 69 (1954): 313-315.

121. Gaylord, A. T. "Friendship in Chaucer's *Troilus,*" *ChauR,* 3 (1969): 239-264.

122. Gaylord, A. T. "Gentilesse in Chaucer's *Troilus,*" *SP,* 61 (1964): 19-34.

123. Gaylord, A. T. "Uncle Pandarus as Lady Philosophy," *PMASAL,* 46 (1961): 571-595.

124. Gill, Sister B. A. *Paradoxical Patterns in Chaucer's Troilus: an Explanation of the Palinode.* Washington, D. C., 1960.

125. Gordon, I. L. *The Double Sorrow of Troilus: a Study of Ambiguities in Troilus and Criseyde.* Oxford, 1970.

126. Gordon, I. L. "The Narrative Function of Irony in Chaucer's *Troilus and Criseyde,*" in *Medieval Miscellany, Presented to Eugène Vinaver,* ed. by F. Whitehead, A. H. Diverres and F. E. Sutcliffe. Manchester, 1965, pp. 146-156.

127. Gray, B. J. "Thematic Opposition of Fortuna and Natura in Chaucer's Narratives," *DA,* 23 (1963): 2517 (Tulane).

128. Green, M. N. "Christian Implications of Knighthood and Courtly Love in Chaucer's *Troilus,*" *DelN,* 30 (1957): 57-92.

129. Greenfield, S. B. "The Role of Calkas in *Troilus and Criseyde,*" *MAE,* 36 (1967): 141-151.

130. Greer, A. W. "Chaucer's *Troilus and Criseyde:* the Tragicomic Dilemma," *DA,* 26 (1966): 4627-28 (U. of Florida).

131. Hagopian, J. V. "Chaucer as Psychologist in *Troilus and Criseyde,*" *L&P,* 5 (1955):5-11.

132. Hammerle, K. "Das Fortunamotiv von Chaucer bis Bacon," *Anglia,* 65 (1941): 87-100.

133. Howard, D. R. "Literature and Sexuality: Book III of Chaucer's *Troilus,*" *MR,* 8 (1967): 442-456.

134. Howard, D. R. *The Three Temptations: Medieval Man in Search of the World.* Princeton, 1966, pp. 77-160.

135. Howard, E. J. *Geoffrey Chaucer.* TEAS, no. 1. New York, 1964, pp. 105-117, 172-174, and passim.

136. Huber, J. "Troilus' Predestination Soliloquy: Chaucer's Changes from Boethius," *NM,* 66 (1965): 120-125.

137. Hutson, A. E. "Troilus' Confession," *MLN,* 69 (1954): 468-470.

138. Jelliffe, R. A. *Troilus and Criseyde: Studies in Interpretation.* Tokyo, 1956.

139. Jordan, R. M. "The Narrator in Chaucer's *Troilus,*" *ELH,* 25 (1958): 237-257.

140. Kean, P. M. "Chaucer's Dealings with a Stanza of *Il Filostrato* and the Epilogue of *Troilus and Criseyde,*" *MAE,* 33 (1964): 36-46.

141. Kelly, A. "Eleanor of Aquitaine and Her Courts of Love," *Spec,* 12 (1937): 3-19.

142. Kirby, T. A. *Chaucer's Troilus: a Study in Courtly Love,* *LSUSHS,* no. 39. Baton Rouge, 1940.

143. Longo, J. A. "The Double Time Scheme in Book II of Chaucer's *Troilus and Criseyde,*" *MLQ,* 22 (1961): 37-40.

144. Lorrah, J. "The 'Present Eternite' of Chaucer's *Troilus and Criseyde,*" *DA,* 30 (1969): 688A (Florida State).

145. McCall, J. P. "The Trojan Scene in Chaucer's *Troilus,*" *ELH,* 29 (1962): 263-275.

146. McKay, E. M. "The Clash and the Fusion of Medieval and Renaissance Elements in Chaucer's *Troilus,*" *DA,* 19 (1959): 2615-16 (Emory).

147. Mahoney, J. F. "Chaucerian Tragedy and the Christian Tradition," *AnM,* 3 (1962): 81-99.

148. Malarkey, S. "The 'Corones Tweyne': an Interpretation," *Spec,* 38 (1963): 473-478.

149. Markland, M. F. "Pilgrims Errant: the Doubleness of *Troilus and Criseyde,*" *RS,* 33 (1965): 64-77.

150. Mayo, R. D. "The Trojan Background of the *Troilus,*" *ELH,* 9 (1942): 245-256.

151. Meech, S. B. *Design in Chaucer's Troilus.* Syracuse, 1959.

152. Mizener, A. "Character and Action in the Case of Criseyde," *PMLA,* 54 (1939): 65-81.

153. Mogan, J. J., Jr. "Chaucer and the Theme of Mutability," *DA,* 22 (1962): 3669-70 (Louisiana State).

154. Mogan, J. J., Jr. "Futher Aspects of Mutability in Chaucer's *Troilus,*" *PELL,* 1 (1965): 72-77.

155. Nagarajan, S. "The Conclusion to Chaucer's *Troilus and Criseyde,*" *EIC,* 13 (1963): 1-8.

156. Owen, C. A., Jr. "The Problem of Free Will in Chaucer's Narratives," *PQ,* 46 (1967): 433-456.

157. Owen, C. A., Jr. "The Significance of Chaucer's Revisions of *Troilus and Criseyde,*" *MP,* 55 (1957): 1-5.

158. Patch, H. R. "Troilus on Determinism," *Spec,* 6 (1931): 225-243.

159. Reedy, E. K. " 'This Litel Spot of Erthe': Time and 'Trouthe' in Chaucer's *Troilus and Criseyde,*" *DA,* 28 (1967): 1057-A (Yale).

160. Reiss, E. "Troilus and the Failure of Understanding," *MLQ,* 29 (1968): 131-144.

161. Renoir, A. "Criseyde's Two Half Lovers," *OL,* 16 (1961): 239-255.

162. Renoir, A. "Thebes, Troy, Criseyde, and Pandarus: an Instance of Chaucerian Irony," *SN,* 32 (1960): 14-17.

163. Rhys, B. "The Role of the Narrator in Chaucer's *Troilus and Criseyde,*" *DA,* 24 (1964): 3327 (Tulane).

164. Robertson, D. W., Jr. "Chaucerian Tragedy," *ELH,* 19 (1952): 1-37.

165. Robertson, D. W., Jr. *A Preface to Chaucer: Studies in Medieval Perspectives.* Princeton, 1962, pp. 472-502.

166. *Root, R. K., ed. Introduction and Notes to *The Book of Troilus and Criseyde: Edited from All the Known MSS.* Princeton, 1926, xi-lxxxix, pp. 409-565.

167. Russell, N. "Characters and Crowds in Chaucer's *Troilus,*" *N&Q,* 13 (1966): 50-52.

168. Salter, E. "Troilus and Criseyde: a Reconsideration," in *Patterns of Love and Courtesy: Essays in Memory of C. S. Lewis,* ed. by J. Lawlor, London, 1966, pp. 86-106.

169. Sams, H. W. "The Dual Time-Scheme in Chaucer's *Troilus,*" *MLN,* 56 (1941): 94-100.

170. Schaar, C. "Troilus' Elegy and Criseyde's," *SN,* 29 (1952): 185-191.

171. Schoeck, R. J. and J. Taylor, eds. *Chaucer Criticism, Vol. II: Troilus and Criseyde & the Minor Poems.* Notre Dame, 1961.

172. Scott, F. S. "The Seventh Sphere: a Note on *Troilus and Criseyde,*" *MLR,* 51 (1956): 2-5.

173. Shanley, J. L. "The *Troilus* and Christian Love," *ELH,* 6 (1939): 271-281.

174. Shannon, E. F. "Chaucer and Lucan's *Pharsalia,*" *MP,* 16 (1919): 609-614.

175. Sharrock, R. "Second Thoughts: C. S. Lewis on Chaucer's *Troilus,*" *EIC,* 8 (1958): 123-137.

176. Shorter, R. N. "Boethian Philosophy as the Informing Principle in Chaucer's *Troilus and Criseyde*," *DA*, 26 (1965): 359 (Duke).

177. Sims, D. "An Essay at the Logic of *Troilus and Criseyde*," *CQ*, 4 (1969): 125-149.

178. Slaughter, E. E. "Love and Grace in Chaucer's *Troilus*," in *Essays in Honor of Walter Clyde Curry*. Nashville, 1954, pp. 61-76.

179. Soules, E. H. *"Troilus and Criseyde:* a Study in Chaucer's Narrative Technique," *DA*, 26 (1966): 6053 (U. of the Pacific).

180. Stearns, M. W. "Henryson and Chaucer," *MLQ*, 6 (1945): 271-284.

181. Stroud, T. A. "Boethius' Influence on Chaucer's *Troilus, MP*, 49 (1951-52): 1-9.

182. Tatlock, J. S. P. "The Epilog of Chaucer's *Troilus*," *MP*, 18 (1921): 625-659.

183. Tatlock, J. S. P. "The People in Chaucer's *Troilus*," *PMLA*, 56 (1941): 85-104.

184. Thompson, L. F. "Artistry in *Troilus and Criseyde:* a Study of Chronology, Structure, Characterization, and Purpose," *DA*, 20 (1959): 1771 (Lehigh).

185. Wagenknecht, E. *The Personality of Chaucer*. Norman, 1968, pp. 87-94 and *passim*.

186. Wager, W. J. " 'Fleshly Love' in Chaucer's *Troilus*," *MLR*, 34 (1939): 62-66.

187. Wenzel, S. "Chaucer's Troilus of Book IV," *PMLA*, 79 (1964): 542-547.

188. Williams, G. *A New View of Chaucer*. Durham, 1965, pp. 66-81.

189. Witlieb, B. L. "Chaucer's Elysian Fields (*Troilus* IV, 789 f.)," *N&Q*, 16 (1969): 250-251.

190. Young, K. "Chaucer's Renunciation of Love in *Troilus*," *MLN*, 40 (1925): 270-276.

See also 196, 198, 211, 269, 348, 689, 712.

JOHN LYDGATE

Fall of Princes (1430-1440)

191. *Bergen, H., ed. Bibliographical Introduction, Notes and Glossary to *Lydgate's Fall of Princes*. EETS, no. 124. Part 4. London, 1927.

192. Edwards, A. S. G. "Lydgate's *Fall of Princes:* Unrecorded Readings," *N&Q,* 16 (1969): 170-171.

193. Gathercole, P. M. "A Frenchman's Praise of Boccaccio," *Italica,* 40 (1963): 225-230.

194. Gathercole, P. M. "Lydgate's *Fall of Princes* and the French Version of Boccaccio's *De casibus,*" in *Miscellanea di studi e ricerche sul quattrocento francese.* Torino, 1966, pp. 167-178.

195. Gathercole, P. M. "Two Old French Translations of Boccaccio's *De casibus virorum illustrium,*" *MLQ,* 17 (1957): 304-309.

196. Hammond, E. P. "Boethius: Chaucer, Walton, Lydgate," *MLN,* 41 (1926): 534-535.

197. Hammond, E. P. "Lydgate and Coluccio Salutati," *MP,* 25 (1927): 49-57.

198. Long, R. A. "John Heywood, Chaucer, and Lydgate," *MLN,* 64 (1949): 55-56.

199. Pearsall, D. *John Lydgate.* Charlottesville, 1970, pp. 223-254.

200. Renoir, A. "Attitudes Toward Women in Lydgate's Poetry," *ES,* 42 (1961): 1-14.

201. Renoir, A. *The Poetry of John Lydgate.* Cambridge, Mass., 1967, *passim.*

202. Schirmer, W. F. "The Importance of the 15th Century for the Study of the English Renaissance," in *English Studies Today: Papers Read at the International Conference of University Professors of English, Oxford, August, 1950,* ed. by C. L. Wrenn and G. Bullough. Oxford, 1951, pp. 104-110.

203. Schirmer, W. F. *John Lydgate: a Study in the Culture of the Fifteenth Century,* trans. by A. E. Keep. Berkeley, 1961, pp. 206-227.

204. Schirmer, W. F. "Lydgate's *Fall of Princes,*" *Anglia,* 69 (1950): 301-334.

See also 32, 42, 222, 689, 699, 738.

ROBERT HENRYSON

Testament of Cresseid (c. 1460)

205. Aswell, E. D. "The Role of Fortune in the *Testament of Cressid," PQ,* 46 (1967): 471-487.

206. Bullough, G. "The Lost *Troilus and Cressida," E&S,* 17 (1964): 24-40.

207. Chessell, D. "In the Dark Time: Henryson's *Testament of Cresseid," CR,* 12 (1969): 61-72.

208. Cogswell, F., Jr. *The Testament of Cresseid.* Toronto, 1957.

209. Duncan, D. "Henryson's *Testament of Cresseid," EIC,* 11 (1961): 128-135.

210. Elliott, C. "Two Notes on Henryson's *Testament of Cresseid," JEGP,* 54 (1955): 241-254.

211. *Fox, D., ed. Introduction and Notes to the *Testament of Cresseid.* London, 1968.

212. Harth, S. J. "Convention and Creation in the Poetry of Robert Henryson: a Study of the *Testament of Cresseid* and *Orpheus and Eurydice.*" Ph.D. Thesis. Chicago, 1961.

213. Hume, K. "Leprosy or Syphilis in Henryson's *Testament of Cresseid," ELN,* 6 (1969): 242-245.

214. Larkey, S. V. "Leprosy in Medieval Romance: a Note on Robert Henryson's *Testament of Cresseid," Bull. Hist. Med.,* 35 (1961): 77-80.

215. McDermott, J. J. "Henryson's *Testament of Cresseid* and Heywood's *A Woman Killed with Kindness," RenQ,* 20 (1967): 16-21.

216. MacQueen, J. *Robert Henryson: a Study of the Major Narrative Poems.* Oxford, 1967, pp. 45-93.

217. Moran, T. "The Meeting of the Lovers in the *Testament of Cresseid," N&Q,* 10 (1963): 11-12.

218. Moran, T. "The *Testament of Cresseid* and the *Book of Troylus," Litera,* 6 (1960): 18-24.

219. Parr, J. "Cresseid's Leprosy Again," *MLN,* 60 (1945): 487-491.

220. Rowland, B. "The 'Seiknes Incurabill' in Henryson's *Testament of Cresseid," ELN,* 1 (1964): 175-177.

221. Spearing, A. C. "The *Testament of Cresseid* and the 'High Concise Style'," *Spec*, 37 (1962): 208-225.

222. Stearns, M. W. "A Note on Henryson and Lydgate," *MLN*, 60 (1945): 101-103.

223. Stearns, M. W. "The Planet Portraits of Robert Henryson," *PMLA*, 59 (1944): 911-927.

224. Stearns, M. W. "Robert Henryson and the Fulgentian Horse," *MLN*, 54 (1939): 239-245.

225. Stearns, M. W. "Robert Henryson and the Leper Cresseid," *MLN*, 59 (1944): 265-269.

226. Toliver, H. E. "Robert Henryson: from *Moralitas* to Irony," *ES*, 46 (1965), 300-309.

227. Whiting, B. J. "A Probable Allusion to Henryson's *Testament of Cresseid*," *MLR*, 40 (1945): 46-47.

Myrroure for Magistrates (1559-1587)

228. Bühler, C. F. "A Survival from the Middle Ages: William Baldwin's Use of the *Dictes and Sayings*," *Spec*, 23 (1948): 76-80.

229. Bush, D. "Classical Lives in the *Mirror for Magistrates*," *SP*, 22 (1925): 256-266.

230. Camp, T. W. "Another Version of 'The Things That Cause a Quiet Lyfe'," *MLN*, 52 (1937): 186-188.

231. Campbell, L. B. "Humphrey Duke of Gloucester and Elianor Cobham His Wife in the *Mirror for Magistrates*," *Huntington Library Bulletin*, no. 5 (1934): 119-155.

232. *Campbell, L. B., ed. Introduction to the *Mirror for Magistrates*. New York, 1960 (Cambridge, 1938), pp. 3-60.

233. Campbell, L. B. *"A Mirror for Magistrates*," *TLS*, June 30, 1932, p. 480.

234. Campbell, L. B. *"A Mirror for Magistrates*," *TLS*, Feb. 29, 1936, p. 188.

235. *Campbell, L. B., ed. *Parts Added to the Mirror for Magistrates by John Higgins and Thomas Blenerhasset*. Huntington Library Publications. Cambridge, 1946.

236. Campbell, L. B. "The Suppressed Edition of *A Mirror for Magistrates*," *Huntington Library Bulletin*, 6 (1934): 1-16.

237. Campbell, L. B. "Tudor Conceptions of History and Tragedy in *A Mirror for Magistrates.*" University of California Faculty Research Lecture. Berkeley, 1935.

238. Capra, C. "Il *Ricardo III* di Shakespeare e il *Mirror for Magistrates,*" *EM,* 13 (1962): 31-58.

239. Cunliffe, J. W. *"A Mirror for Magistrates,"* in *The Cambridge History of English Poetry.* Vol. 3. Cambridge, 1930, pp. 192-200.

240. Davies, G. *"Mirror for Magistrates,"* *TLS,* July 23, 1931, p. 583.

241. Duncan, T. G. "Notes on the Language of the Hunterian Manuscript of the *Mirror,*" *NM,* 69 (1968): 204-208.

242. Farnham, W. "John Higgins' *Mirror* and *Locrine,*" *MP,* 23 (1926): 307-313.

243. Farnham, W. "The *Mirror for Magistrates* and Elizabethan Tragedy," *JEGP,* 25 (1926): 66-78.

244. Farnham, W. "The Progeny of *A Mirror for Magistrates,*" *MP,* 29 (1932): 395-410.

245. Feasey, E. I. "The Licensing of the *Mirror for Magistrates,*" *Library,* 3 (1922): 177-193.

246. Feasey, E. I. "William Baldwin," *MLR,* 20 (1925): 407-418.

247. Hearsey, M., ed. *The Complaint of Henry Duke of Buckingham, including the Induction, or Thomas Sackville's Contribution to the Mirror for Magistrates.* YSE, no. 86. New Haven, 1936.

248. Hearsey, M. "The MS of Sackville's Contribution to the *Mirror for Magistrates,*" *RES,* 8 (1932): 282-290.

249. Hogue, L. L. "Sackville's 'The Complaint of Henry, Duke of Buckingham, 58'," *Expl,* 28 (1969): Item 8.

250. Howarth, R. G. "Thomas Sackville and *A Mirror for Magistrates,*" *ESA,* 6 (1963): 77-99.

251. Jackson, W. A. "Wayland's Edition of the *Mirror for Magistrates,*" *Library,* 13 (1932): 155-157.

252. Kinsman, R. S. " 'A Lamentable of Kyng Edward the IIII'," *HLQ,* 29 (1966): 95-108.

253. Lievsay, J. L. "Order and Decorum in *A Mirror for Magistrates,*" *TSL,* 2 (1957): 87-93.

254. Martin, B. C. *"Shore's Wife* as a Source of the Epilogue to *Dr. Faustus,"* *N&Q,* 195 (1951): 182.

255. Parker, D. *"A Mirror for Magistrates,"* *Contemporary Review,* no. 1128 (1960): 41-44.

256. Peery, W. "A Metrical Puzzle in the *Mirror for Magistrates,"* *MLN,* 56 (1941): 258-261.

257. Peery, W. "Tragic Retribution in the 1559 *Mirror for Magistrates,"* *SP,* 46 (1949): 113-130.

258. "A Poet Turned Statesman. Sir Thomas Sackville in Court and Study," *TLS,* January 25, 1936, pp. 61-62.

259. Pyle, F. *"A Mirror for Magistrates,"* *TLS,* Dec. 28, 1935, p. 904.

260. Pyle, F. "Thomas Sackville and *A Mirror for Magistrates,"* *RES,* 14 (1938): 315-321.

261. Rowse, A. L. *"Mirror for Magistrates,"* *TLS,* April 15, 1939, p. 217.

262. Taylor, M. A. "Lord Cobham and the *Mirror for Magistrates,"* *SAB,* 8 (1933): 154-160.

263. Thaler, A. "Literary Criticism in *A Mirror for Magistrates,"* *JEGP,* 49 (1950): 1-13.

264. Tillyard, E. M. W. *"A Mirror for Magistrates* Revisited," in *Elizabethan and Jacobean Studies,* ed. by H. Davis and H. Gardner. Oxford, 1960, pp. 1-16.

265. Weaver, J. J. "Rhetoric and Tragedy in Thomas Sackville's Contributions to the *Mirror for Magistrates,"* *DA,* 29 (1969): 3162A (Ohio State).

See also 294, 300, 347, 348, 352, 690, 699, 738.

GEORGE CAVENDISH

Metrical Visions (c. 1550-1560)

266. *Fisher, M. R. "George Cavendish's *Metrical Visions,"* *DA,* 28 (1968): 5014A (Columbia).

267. Rossi, S. "George Cavendish e il Tema della Fortuna," *EM,* 9 (1958): 51-76.

See also 699, 738.

EDMUND SPENSER

The Ruines of Time [*Complaints*] (1591)

268. Bayley, P. C. "Order, Grace and Courtesy in Spenser's World," in *Patterns of Love and Courtesy: Essays in Memory of C. S. Lewis,* ed. by J. Lawlor. London, 1966, pp. 178-202.

269. Cawley, R. R. "A Chaucerian Echo in Spenser," *MLN,* 41 (1926): 313-314.

270. Clements, R. J. "Iconography on the Nature and Inspiration of Poetry in Renaissance Emblem Literature," *PMLA,* 70 (1955): 781-804.

271. Harrison, T. P., Jr. "Spenser and the Earlier Pastoral Elegy," *Studies in English, University of Texas,* 13 (1933): 36-53.

272. Nelson, W. *The Poetry of Edmund Spenser: a Study.* New York, 1963, pp. 64-83.

273. *Osgood, C. G., H. G. Lotspeich, eds., assisted by D. E. Mason. Notes to *The Ruines of Time,* in *The Works of Edmund Spenser: a Variorum Edition; The Minor Poems, Vol. II,* ed. by E. Greenlaw, et al. Baltimore, 1947, pp. 283-310, 521-530.

274. Osgood, C. G. "Spenser's English Rivers," *Transactions of the Connecticut Academy of Arts and Sciences,* 23 (1920): 65-108.

275. Pienaar, W. J. B. "Spenser's *Complaints,*" *TLS,* December 4, 1924, p. 825.

276. Stein, H. *Studies in Spenser's Complaints.* New York, 1934.

SAMUEL DANIEL

The Complaint of Rosamond [*Delia*] (1592)

The Ciuile Wars between the Two Houses of Lancaster and Yorke (1595)

277. Adamany, R. G. "Daniel's Debt to Foreign Literatures and *Delia* Edited," *DA,* 23 (1963): 4350-51 (U. of Wisconsin).

278. Carson, N. M. "The Literary Reputation of Samuel Daniel," *DA,* 23 (1963): 1683 (Boston).

279. Chang, J. S. "Machiavellianism in Daniel's *The Civil Wars,*" *TSE,* 14 (1965): 5-16.

280. Goldman, L. "Samuel Daniel's *Delia* and the Emblem Tradition," *JEGP*, 67 (1968): 49-63.

281. *Grosart, A. B., ed. *Complete Works in Verse and Prose of Samuel Daniel*. 5 vols. London, 1885-96.

282. Law, R. A. "Daniel's *Rosamond* and Shakespeare," *Studies in English, University of Texas* (1947): 42-48.

283. *Michel, L., ed. Introduction to *The Civil Wars by Daniel*. New Haven, 1958, pp. 1-62.

284. Michel, L. " 'Sommers Heate' Again," *N&Q*, 195 (1950): 292-293.

285. Miller, E. H. "Samuel Daniel's Revisions in *Delia*," *JEGP*, 53 (1954): 58-68.

286. Rees, J. *Samuel Daniel: a Critical and Biographical Study*. Liverpool English Texts and Studies, no. 9. Liverpool, 1964, pp. 13-42.

287. Schaar, C. *An Elizabethan Sonnet Problem: Shakespeare's Sonnets, Daniel's Delia, and Their Literary Background, LSE*, no. 28. Lund & Copenhagen, 1960.

288. Schaar, C. "A Textual Puzzle in Daniel's *Delia*," *ES*, 40 (1959): 382-385.

289. Seronsy, C. C. "Daniel's *Complaint of Rosamond:* Origins and Influence of an Elizabethan Poem," *LHB*, 2 (1960): 39-57.

290. Seronsy, C. C. *Samuel Daniel. TEAS*, no. 49. New York, 1967, pp. 33-41, 61-78, *passim*.

291. Seronsy, C. C. and R. Krueger. "A Manuscript of Daniel's *Civil Wars*, Book III," *SP*, 63 (1966): 157-162.

292. Williamson, C. F. "The Design of Daniel's *Delia*," *RES*, 19 (1968): 251-260.

See also 300, 303, 520, 524, 536, 699.

THOMAS LODGE

The Tragicall Complaynt of Elstred [Phillis] (1593)

293. *Gosse, E., ed. *The Complete Works of Thomas Lodge*. 4 vols. Edinburgh, 1875-88, 1963.

294. Rae, W. D. *Thomas Lodge*. TEAS, no. 59. New York, 1967, pp. 82, 37-39.

See also 244, 699.

GILES FLETCHER (the elder)

The Rising to the Crowne of Richard the Third (1593)

295. *Berry, L. E., ed. Introduction to the *Rising to the Crowne of Richard the Third* in *The English Works of Giles Fletcher, the Elder*. Madison, 1964, pp. 64-72.

See also 244, 738.

THOMAS CHURCHYARD

Shores Wife [Churchyardes Challenge] (1593)

296. Geimer, R. A. "The Life and Works of Thomas Churchyard," *DA*, 26 (1965): 3302 (Northwestern).

297. *Rahter, C. A. "A Critical Edition of *Churchyard's Challenge* (1593) by Thomas Churchyard, with Some Notes on the Author's Life and Works," *DA*, 18 (1958): 1794-95 (U. of Pennsylvania).

298. Rahter, C. A. "Some Notes on the Career and Personality of Thomas Churchyard," *N&Q*, 7 (1960): 211-215.

299. St. Onge, H. O. "Thomas Churchyard: a Study of His Prose and Poetry," *DA*, 27 (1967): 3849A-50A (Ohio State).

See also 244, 254, 699, 738.

MICHAEL DRAYTON

Piers Gaueston, Earle of Cornwall (c. 1594)

Matilda (1594)

The Tragicall Legend of Robert, Duke of Normandy (1596)

The Barons Warres [Mortimeriados rewritten] (1603, 1596)

300. Berthelot, J. A. *Michael Drayton*. TEAS, no. 52. New York, 1967, pp. 71-93.

301. *Hebel, J. W., et al., eds. *The Complete Works of Michael Drayton*. 5 vols. Oxford, 1931-41.

302. Hebel, J. W. "The Surreptitious Editions of Michael Drayton's *Peirs Gaueston*," *Library*, 4 (1923): 151-155.

303. LaBranche, A. "Drayton's *The Barons Warres* and the Rhetoric of Historical Poetry," *JEGP,* 62 (1963): 82-95.

304. Praz, M. "Michael Drayton," *ES,* 28 (1947): 97-107.

See also 244, 699, 738.

II. DRAMATIC TRAGEDY

II. DRAMATIC TRAGEDY

JOHN SKELTON

Magnyfycence (c. 1516)

305. Carpenter, N. C. *John Skelton. TEAS,* no. 61, New York, 1967.

306. Green, P. *John Skelton.* Writers and Their Work, no. 128. London, 1960.

307. Harris, W. O. *Skelton's Magnyfycence and the Cardinal Virtue Tradition.* Chapel Hill, 1965.

308. Harris, W. O. "The Thematic Importance of Skelton's Allusion to Horace in *Magnyfycence," SEL,* 3 (1963): 9-18.

309. Harris, W. O. "Wolsey and Skelton's *Magnyfycence:* a Re-Valuation," *SP* 62 (1960): 99-122.

310. *Henderson, P., ed. The Complete Poems of John Skelton.* London & Toronto, 1931.

311. Kinsman, R. S. "Skelton's *Magnyfycence:* the Strategy of the 'Olde Sayde Sawe'," *SP,* 63 (1966): 99-125.

312. Phillips, N. A. "John Skelton and the Tradition of English Realism," *DA,* 28 (1968): 2653-A (Yale).

313. Phillips, N. A. "Observations on the Derivation Method of Skelton's Realism," *JEGP,* 65 (1966): 19-35.

314. Pollet, M. *John Skelton.* Contribution a l'histoire de la pre-renaissance anglaise. Paris, 1962.

315. Rowland, B. " 'Bone-Ache' in Skelton's *Magnyfycence," N&Q,* 11 (1964): 211.

THOMAS WATSON

Absalom (1535-1544)

316. Barnfield, R. "Amyntas and the Sidney Circle," *PMLA,* 74 (1959): 318-324 (Reply by W. Staton and H. Morris. "Thomas Watson and Abraham Fraunce," *PMLA,* 76 (1961): 150-153).

317. Eccles, M. *Christopher Marlowe in London.* Cambridge, Mass., 1934, pp. 128-132 and *passim.*

318. Morris, B. R. "Thomas Watson and Troilus and Cressida," *N&Q,* 5 (1958): 198-199. Reprinted, pp. 244-245.

319. Smith, J. H. "Thomas Watson's *Absalom,* an Edition, Translation, and Critical Study," *DA,* 18 (1958): 2149-2150 (U. of Illinois).

320. *Smith, J. H., ed. *Absalom.* ISLL, vol. 52. Urbana, 1964.

See also 472.

JOHN BALE

The Chief Promyses of God unto Man (1538)

Kynge Johan (c. 1540)

321. Adams, B. B. "Doubling in Bale's *King Johan,"* SP, 62 (1965): 111-120.

322. Adams, B. B. "John Bale's *King Johan,* edited with an Introduction and Notes," *DA,* 25 (1965): 4696 (U. of North Carolina, 1963).

323. Barke, H. *Bales Kynge Johan und sein Verhältnis zur zeit-genössischen Geschichtsschreibung.* Würzburg, 1937.

324. Cason, C. E. "Additional Lines for Bale's *Kynge Johan,"* JEGP, 27 (1928): 42-50.

325. Davies, W. T. "A Bibliography of John Bale," *Oxford Bibliographical Society Proceedings and Papers,* 5 (1939): 201-279.

326. Elson, J. "Studies in the King John Plays," *Joseph Quincy Adams Memorial Studies,* ed. by J. G. McManaway, G. E. Dawson, and E. E. Willoughby. Washington, 1948, pp. 183-197.

327. *Farmer, J. S., ed. *The Dramatic Writings of John Bale.* London, 1907.

328. Greg, W. W. "Bale's *Kynge Johan,*" *MLN,* 36 (1921): 505.

329. Harris, J. W. *John Bale: a Study in the Minor Literature of the Reformation,* ISLL, no. 25. Urbana, 1940.

330. Harris, J. W. *The Life and Works of John Bale, 1495-1563.* Ph.D. Thesis. U. of Illinois, 1935.

331. Le Boutillier, M. "Bale's *Kynge Johan* and the *Troublesome Raigne,*" *MLN,* 36 (1921): 55-57.

332. Miller, E. "The Roman Rite in Bale's *King John,*" *PMLA,* 64 (1949): 802-822.

333. Mozley, J. F. "John Bale," *N&Q,* 189 (1945): 276-277.

334. Pafford, J. H. P. "Bale's *King John,*" *JEGP,* 30 (1931): 176-178.

335. Pafford, J. H. P. "Two Notes on Bale's *King John,*" *MLR,* 56 (1961): 553-555.

See also 678, 699, 720.

GEORGE BUCHANAN

Baptistes (c. 1541)

Jephthes (c. 1554)

336. Hadas, M. "George Buchanan, Scottish Humanist," *SAQ,* 43 (1944): 390-395.

See also 769, 771.

NICHOLAS GRIMALD

Archipropheta (1547-1548)

Christus Redivivus (1543)

337. Abel, P. "Grimald's *Christus Redivivus* and the Digby Resurrection Play," *MLN,* 70 (1955): 328-330.

338. Blackburn, R. H. "Nicholas Grimald's *Christus Redivivus:* a Protestant Resurrection Play," *ELN,* 5 (1968): 247-250.

339. Hudson, H. H. "Grimald's Translations from Beza," *MLN,* 39 (1924): 388-394.

340. *Merrill, L. R., ed. *The Life and Poems of Nicholas Grimald.* Yale Studies in English, no. 69, New Haven, 1925.

341. Taylor, G. C. "The *Christus Redivivus* of Nicholas Grimald and the Hegge Resurrection Plays," *PMLA,* 41 (1926): 840-859.

JOHN PHILLIPS

Pacient and Meeke Grissill (1558-1561)

342. Roberts, C. W. "An Edition of John Phillip's *Commodye of Pacient and Meeke Grissil,*" Ph.D. Thesis. U. of Illinois, 1938.

343. Swaen, A. E. H. "The Songs in John Phillip's *Patient Grissell,*" *Archiv,* 168 (1935): 77-79.

See also 699.

WILLIAM WAGER

The Longer Thou Livest, the More Fool Thou Art (c. 1559)

Inough Is as Good as a Feast (c. 1560)

344. Benbow, R. M., ed. *The Longer Thou Livest and Enough Is as Good as a Feast. RRDS.* Lincoln, 1967.

See also 496, 699, 720.

THOMAS SACKVILLE AND THOMAS NORTON

Gorboduc (1562)

345. Bacquet, P. "L'influence de Sénèque sur *Gorboduc,*" *EA,* 14 (1961): 344-345.

346. Bacquet, P. "Le moyen âge anglais et les idées morales de Thomas Sackville," *BFLS,* 42 (1964): 437-445.

347. Bacquet, P. *Thomas Sackville: L'homme et l'œuvre.* Travaux d'humanisme et renaissance, no. 76. Genève, 1966, *passim.*

348. Baker, H. *Induction to Tragedy. A Study in a Development of Form in Gorboduc, the Spanish Tragedy, and Titus Andronicus.* Baton Rouge, La., 1939.

349. Carneiro de Mendonca, B. H. "The Influence of *Gorboduc* on *King Lear*," *ShS,* 13 (1960): 41-48.

350. Cauthen, I. B., Jr. *"Gorboduc, Ferrex and Porrex:* the First Two Quartos," *SB,* 15 (1962), 231-233.

351. *Cunliffe, J. W., ed. *Gorboduc,* in *Early English Classical Tragedies.* Oxford, 1912.

352. Hearsey, M. "Thomas Sackville," *TLS,* April 18, 1929, p. 315.

353. Herrick, M. T. "Senecan Influence in *Gorboduc*," in *Studies in Speech and Drama in Honor of Alexander M. Drummond.* Ithaca, 1944, pp. 78-105.

354. Johnson, S. F. *"Gorboduc* and Howell, His Devises (1581)," *N&Q,* 196 (1951): 452.

355. Peters, R. A. *"Gorboduc* and Grafton's *Chronicle*," *N&Q,* 4 (1957): 333.

356. Small, S. A. "The Political Import of the Norton Half of *Gorboduc*," *PMLA,* 46 (1931): 641-646.

357. Summerell, J. H. " 'Violence and/or Violins'," *N&Q,* 4 (1957): 419-420.

358. Talbert, E. W. "The Political Import and the First Two Audiences of *Gorboduc*," in *Studies in Honor of DeWitt T. Starnes,* ed. by Harrison, Hill, Mossner and Sledd. Austin, 1967, pp. 89-115.

359. Turner, R. Y. "Pathos and the *Gorboduc* Tradition, 1560-1590," *HLQ,* 35 (1962): 97-120.

360. Walsh, M. "A Critical Edition of *Gorboduc*," *DA,* 25 (1965): 4693 (St. Louis).

361. Watson, S. *"Gorboduc* and the Theory of Tyrrannicide," *MLR,* 34 (1939): 355-366.

See also 248, 249, 250, 258, 260, 265, 348, 699, 718, 720.

GEORGE GASCOIGNE
(AND FRANCES KINWELMERSHE?)

Jocasta (1566)

362. *Cunliffe, J. W., ed. *Jocasta,* in *Early English Classical Tragedies.* Oxford, 1912.

363. Forssberg, C. F. W., Jr. "A Critical Old-Spelling Edition of *Supposes* by George Gascoigne and *Jocasta* by George Gascoigne and Francis Kinwelmarsh with Introduction and Notes," *DA,* 29 (1968): 889-A (Vanderbilt).

364. Modic, J. "Gascoigne and Ariosto Again," *CL,* 14 (1962): 317-319.

See also 718.

CHRISTOPHER HATTON AND ROBERT WILMOT

Gismund of Salerne (1567-1568, revised as *Tancred and Gismund, 1591*)

365. *Cunliffe, J. W., ed. *Gismund of Salerne,* in *Early English Classical Tragedies.* Oxford, 1912. (Wilmot's revision is reprinted by the Malone Society, London, 1914.)

366. Griffin, E. G. *"Gismond of Salerne:* a Critical Appreciation," *REL,* 4 (1963):94-107.

367. Habicht, W. "Die Nutrix-Szenen in *Gismond of Salern* und *Tancred and Gismund:* Zur akademischen Seneca-Nachahmung in England," *Anglia,* 81 (1963): 394-411.

368. Klein, D. "According to the Decorum of These Daies," *PMLA,* 33 (1918): 244-268.

369. Murray, J. J. *"Tancred and Gismund,"* RES, 14 (1938): 385-395.

370. Selden, K. (Iriye). "A Stylistic Comparison of *Gismond of Salerne* and *Tancred and Gismund,"* ShStud, 4 (1966): 1-35.

See also 623, 678, 699, 718, 720.

JOHN PICKERING

A Newe Enterlude of Vice Conteyninge the Historye of Horestes (c. 1567)

371. De Chickera, E. B. *"Horestes' Revenge*—Another Interpretation," *N&Q,* 6 (1959): 190.

372. Happé, P. "Tragic Themes in Three Tudor Moralities," *SEL,* 5 (1965): 207-227.

373. Phillips, J. E. "A Revaluation of *Horestes* (1567)," *HLQ,* 18 (1955): 227-244.

374. *Seltzer, D. and A. Brown, eds. *A Newe Enterlude of Vice* (or *Horestes*). London, 1962.

R. B. (RICHARD BOWER?)

Appius and Virginia (c. 1559-1567)

375. Clark, A. M. "The Authorship of *Appius and Virginia*," *MLR*, 16 (1921): 1-17.

376. Dickens, L. G. "The Story of Appius and Virginia in English Literature," *DA*, 24 (1963): 2011-2012 (U. of Rochester).

377. Ekeblad, I —S. "Storm Imagery in *Appius and Virginia*," *N&Q*, 3 (1956): 5-7.

378. *McKerrow, R. B., ed. *Appius and Virginia*. London, 1911.

See also 496, 720.

ULPIAN FULWELL

Like Will to Like (1568)

379. *Farmer, J. S., ed. *The Dramatic Writings of Ulpian Fulwell*. New York, 1966 (1906).

380. Sabol, A. J. "A Three-Man Song in Fulwell's *Like Will to Like* at the Folger," *RN*, 10 (1957): 139-142.

See also 496, 699.

THOMAS PRESTON

Cambises King of Persia (c. 1569)

381. *Adams, J. Q., ed. *Cambises*, in *Chief Pre-Shakespearean Dramas*. Boston, 1924.

382. Allen, D. C. "A Source for *Cambises*," *MLN*, 49 (1934): 384-387.

383. Armstrong, W. A. "The Authorship and Political Meaning of *Cambises*," *ES*, 36 (1955): 289-299.

384. Armstrong, W. A. "The Background and Sources of Preston's *Cambises*," *ES*, 31 (1950): 129-135.

385. Feldman, A. "King Cambises' Vein," *N&Q*, 196 (1951): 98-100.

386. Johnson, R. C. "Antedatings from *Cambises*," *N&Q*, 15 (1968): 246.

387. Johnson, R. C. "Press Variants in *Cambises*," *N&Q*, 15 (1968): 246-247.

388. Johnson, R. C. "The Third Quarto of *Cambises*," *N&Q*, 15 (1968): 247.

389. Johnson, R. C. "Thomas Preston's *Cambises:* a Critical Edition," *DA*, 25 (1965): 4688 (U. of Illinois).

390. Linthicum, M. C. "The Date of *Cambyses*," *PMLA*, 49 (1934): 959-961.

391. Starnes, D. T. "Richard Taverner's the *Garden of Wisdom*, Carion's *Chronicles*, and the Cambyses Legend," *Studies in English, University of Texas*, 35 (1956): 22-31.

See also 372, 699, 720.

THOMAS LEGGE

Richardus Tertius (1579-1580)

392. *Collier, J. P. and W. C. Hazlitt, eds. *Richardus Tertius*, in *Shakespeare's Library*. 6 vols. 1875.

393. Lordi, R. J. "The Relationship of *Richardus Tertius* to the Main Richard III Plays," *BUSE*, 5 (1961): 139-153.

394. Lordi, R. J. "Thomas Legge's *Richardus Tertius:* a Critical Edition with a Translation," *DA*, 18 (1958): 1787 (U. of Illinois).

See also 699, 720.

WILLIAM GAGER

Ulysses Redux (c. 1580)

Meleager (c. 1581)

Dido (1583)

Oedipus (c. 1584)

395. Baytop, A. A. "Rhetoric for *Dulce* and *Utile:* William Gager's Critical and Dramatic Practice," *DA*, 27 (1966): 3861-A-3862-A (U. of Massachusetts).

396. Bowers, R. H. "William Gager's *Oedipus*," *SP*, 46 (1949): 141-153.

397. Brooke, C. F. T. "The Life and Times of William Gager (1555-1622)," *PAPS*, 95 (1951): 401-431.

398. Henley, E. F. "A Little-Known Phase in English Drama: William Gager's *Ulysses Redux,*" *LangQ,* 2 (1964): 13-18.

399. *Henley, E. F. "William Gager's *Ulysses Redux* (1592): a Facsimile Edition and an English Translation," *DA,* 23 (1962): 1186 (Florida State).

400. Salter, H. E. "William Gager," *TLS,* May 2, 1936, p. 379.

THOMAS KYD

The Spanish Tragedy (1585-1589)

Soliman and Perseda (1582-1592)

401. Adams, B. B. "The Audiences of the *Spanish Tragedy,*" *JEGP,* 68 (1969): 221-236.

402. Alexander, J. "Parallel Tendencies in English and Spanish Tragedy in the Renaissance," *Studies in Comparative Literature,* Humanistics Series 11. Baton Rouge, La., 1962, pp. 84-101.

403. Baker, H. "Ghosts and Guides: Kyd's *Spanish Tragedy* and the Medieval Tragedy," *MP,* 32 (1935): 27-36.

404. Baldwin, T. W. "On the Chronology of Thomas Kyd's Works," *MLN,* 40 (1925): 343-349.

405. Baldwin, T. W. "Parallels Between *Soliman and Perseda* and Garnier's *Bradamante,*" *MLN,* 51 (1936): 237-241.

406. Bercovitch, S. "Love and Strife in Kyd's *Spanish Tragedy,*" *SEL,* 9 (1969): 215-229.

407. Biesterfeldt, P. W. *Die dramatische Technik Thomas Kyds.* Halle, 1936.

408. *Boas, F. S., ed. *The Works of Thomas Kyd.* Oxford, 1901.

409. Bowers, F. T. "Kyd's Pedringano: Sources and Parallels," *Harvard Studies and Notes in Philology and Literature,* 13 (1931): 241-249.

410. Bowers, F. T. "A Note on the *Spanish Tragedy,*" *MLN,* 53 (1938): 590-591.

411. Butrym, A. "A Marlowe Echo in Kyd," *N&Q,* 5 (1958): 96-97.

412. Cairncross, A. S. "Thomas Kyd and the Myrmidons," *ArlQ,* 1 (1968): 40-45.

413. *Cairncross, A. S., ed. Thomas Kyd, [*The Spanish Comedy, or*] *The First Part of Hieronomo* and *The Spanish Tragedy* [or *Hieronomo is Mad Again*], Lincoln, 1967, pp. xi-xxxiii.

414. Cannon, C. K. "The Relation of the Additions of the *Spanish Tragedy* to the Original Play," *SEL,* 2 (1962): 229-239.

415. Coursen, H. R., Jr. "The Unity of the *Spanish Tragedy*," *SP,* 65 (1968): 768-782.

416. Crundell, H. W. "The 1602 Additions To The *Spanish Tragedy*," *N&Q,* 164 (1933): 147-149 (reply by Howarth, 166 (1934): 246, rejoinder by Crundell, 167 (1934): 88, and again in 180 (1941): 8-9).

417. De Chickera, E. B. "Divine Justice and Private Revenge in the Spanish Tragedy," *MLR,* 57 (1962): 228-232.

418. Dudrap, C. "La *Tragedie espagnole* face a la critique elisa-bethaine et jacobeenne," *Dramaturgie et societe: Rapports entre l'oeuvre theatracle, son interpretation et son public aux xvi*ᵉ *et xvii*ᵉ *siecles,* ed. by Jacquot, Konigson, Oddon. Paris, 1968, pp. 607-631.

419. Edwards, P. *Thomas Kyd and Early Elizabethan Tragedy.* Writers and Their Work, no. 192. London, 1966.

420. Empson, W. "The *Spanish Tragedy*," *Nimbus,* 3 (1956): 16-29 (reprinted in *Elizabethan Drama: Modern Essays in Criticism,* ed. R. J. Kaufmann. New York, 1961, pp. 60-81).

421. Forsythe, R. "Notes on the *Spanish Tragedy*," *PQ,* 5 (1926): 78-84.

422. Freeman, A. "New Records of Thomas Kyd and His Family," *N&Q,* 12 (1965): 328-329.

423. Freeman, A. "Shakespeare and *Solyman and Perseda*," *MLR,* 58 (1963): 481-487.

424. Freeman, A. "The Printing of the *Spanish Tragedy*," *Library* 24 (1969): 187-199.

425. Freeman, A. *Thomas Kyd: Facts and Problems.* Oxford, 1967.

426. Fuzier, J. "Carriere et popularite de la *Tragedie espagnole* en Angleterre," in *Dramaturgie et societe,* ed by Jacquot, Konigson, Oddon. Paris, 1968, pp. 589-606.

427. Fuzier, J. "Thomas Kyd et l'ethique du spectacle populaire," *LanM,* 59 (1965): 451-458.

428. Goodstein, P. "Hieronimo's Destruction of Babylon," *ELN,* 3 (1966): 172-173.

429. Gray, H. D. "Reconstruction of a Lost Play," *PQ,* 7 (1928): 254-274.

430. Greg, W. W. "The *Spanish Tragedy*—a Leading Case?" *Library,* 6 (1925): 47-56.

431. Grubb, M. "Kyd's Borrowing from Garnier's *Bradamante,*" *MLN,* 50 (1935): 169-171.

432. Hapgood, R. "The Judge in the Firie Tower: Another Virgilian Passage in the *Spanish Tragedy,*" *N&Q,* 13 (1966): 287-288.

433. Heyningen, C. "The Additions to Kyd's *Spanish Tragedy,*" *Theoria,* 17 (1961): 38-53.

434. Hunter, G. K. "Ironies of Justice in the *Spanish Tragedy,*" *RenD,* 8 (1965): 89-104.

435. Jensen, E. J. "Kyd's *Spanish Tragedy:* the Play Explains Itself," *JEGP,* 64 (1965): 7-16.

436. Johnson, S. F. "The *Spanish Tragedy,* or Babylon Revisited," in *Essays on Shakespeare and the Elizabethan Drama in Honor of Hardin Craig.* Columbia, Mo., 1962, pp. 23-36.

437. Kirschbaum, L. "Is the *Spanish Tragedy* a Leading Case? Did a Bad Quarto of *Love's Labour's Lost* Ever Exist?" *JEGP,* 37 (1938): 501-512.

438. Laird, D. "Hieronimo's Dilemma," *SP,* 62 (1965): 137-146.

439. Levin, H. "An Echo from the *Spanish Tragedy,*" *MLN,* 64 (1949): 297-302.

440. Levin, M. H. " 'Vindicta Mihi!': Meaning, Morality and Motivation in the *Spanish Tragedy,*" *SEL,* 4 (1964): 307-324.

441. Maxwell, J. C. "Kyd's *Spanish Tragedy,* III. xiv. 168-169, *PQ,* 30 (1951): 86.

442. *Murray, J. J. "The *Tragedye of Solyman and Perseda.* Edited from the Original Texts with Introduction and Notes," *DA,* 20 (1959): 3284 (New York University).

443. Mustard, W. P. "Notes on Thomas Kyd's Works," *PQ,* 5 (1926): 85-86.

444. Pal, R. "Thomas Kyd: the *Spanish Tragedy,* the Establishment of a Tradition in Elizabethan Tragedy," *Agra University Journal of Research,* 11 (1963): 67-88.

445. Plard, H. "Adaptations de la *Tragedie espagnole* dans les Pays-Bas et en Allemagne (1595-1640)," *Dramaturgie et societe,* ed. by Jacquot, Konigson, Oddon. Paris, 1968, pp. 633-653.

446. Price, H. T. *"Titus Andronicus* and the Additions to the *Spanish Tragedy,"* N&Q, 9 (1962): 331.

447. Ratliff, J. D. "Hieronimo Explains Himself," *SP,* 54 (1957): 112-118.

448. Ratliff, J. D. "The Kydian Revenge Play," *DA,* 24 (1954): 2338 (Stanford).

449. Reiman, D. "Marston, Jonson, and the *Spanish Tragedy* Additions," *N&Q,* 7 (1960): 336-337.

450. Ross, T. W. "Kyd's the *Spanish Tragedy:* a Bibliographical Hypothesis," *BRMMLA,* 22 (1968): 13-21.

451. Schaar, C. " 'They Hang Him in the Arbor'," *ES,* 47 (1966): 27-28 (rejoinder by J. L. Smith, pp. 372-373; reply by C. Schaar, p. 373).

452. Schücking, L. L. "The *Spanish Tragedy* Additions. Acting and Reading Versions," *TLS,* June 12, 1937, p. 442.

453. Schücking, L. L. *Zur Verfasserschaft der Spanish Tragedy.* München, 1963.

454. De Smet, J. *Thomas Kyd, l'homme, l'oeuvre, le milieu, suivi de la Tragedie espagnole.* Bruxelles, 1925.

455. Stamm, R. "The Theatrical Physiognomy of the *Spanish Tragedy* and *Hamlet,"* in *English Studies Today,* ed. by I. Cellini and G. Melchiori. Rome, 1966, pp. 137-158.

456. Stoll, E. E. *"Hamlet* and the *Spanish Tragedy.* Quartos I and II: a Protest," *MP,* 35 (1937): 31-46.

457. Wiatt, W. H. "The Dramatic Function of the Alexandro-Villuppo Episode in the *Spanish Tragedy,"* N&Q, 5 (1958): 327-329.

458. Wittig, K. "Gedanken zu Kyd's *Spanish Tragedie,"* *Strena Anglica: Otto Ritter zum 80. Geburtstag.* Halle, 1956.

See also 348, 495, 686, 699, 718, 720, 728, 743, 816.

THOMAS HUGHES

Misfortunes of Arthur (1588)

459. Armstrong, W. A. "Elizabethan Themes in the *Misfortunes of Arthur*," *RES,* 7 (1956): 238-249.

460. Armstrong, W. A. "The Topicality of the *Misfortunes of Arthur*," *N&Q,* 2 (1955): 371-373.

461. Clemen, W. "Anticipation and Foreboding in Shakespeare's Early Histories," *ShS,* 6 (1953): 25-35.

462. *Cunliffe, J. W., ed. *Misfortunes of Arthur,* in *Early English Classical Tragedies.* Oxford, 1912.

463. Logan, G. M. "Hughes's Use of Lucan in the *Misfortunes of Arthur*," *RES,* 20 (1969): 22-32.

464. Maxwell, J. C. "Lucan's First Translator," *N&Q,* 192 (1947): 521-522.

465. Maxwell, J. C. "Seneca in the *Misfortunes of Arthur*," *N&Q,* 7 (1960): 171.

466. Reese, G. "Political Import of the *Misfortunes of Arthur*," *RES,* 21 (1945): 81-89.

467. Waller, E. H. "A Possible Interpretation of the *Misfortunes of Arthur*," *JEGP,* 24 (1925): 219-245.

468. W. J. B. "Thomas Hughes: *Misfortunes of Arthur*," *N&Q,* 159 (1930): 264 (see also the note by A. Sparke on the same page).

See also 348, 686, 720.

THOMAS LODGE

The Wounds of Civill War [Marius and Scilla] (c. 1588)

469. Armstrong, W. A. "Tamburlaine and the *Wounds of Civil War*," *N&Q,* 5 (1958): 381-383.

470. *Houppert, J. W. "An Edition of the *Wounds of Civil War* by Thomas Lodge," *DA,* 25 (1965): 7244 (Michigan).

471. Sorensen, K. "Thomas Lodge's Seneca," *Archiv,* 199 (1962): 313-324.

472. Staton, W. "A Lodge Borrowing from Watson," *RN,* 14 (1961): 3-6.

473. *Wilson, J. D., ed. *Wounds of Civill War*. London, 1910.

See also 293, 294.

GEORGE PEELE

Battell of Alcazar (c. 1589)

Edward I (1593)

Alphonsus, Emperor of Germany (c. 1594)

David and Bethsabe (1599)

474. Ashe, D. "The Text of Peele's *Edward I*," SB, 7 (1955): 153-170.

475. Ekeblad, I-S. "The *Love of King David and Fair Bethsabe:* a Note on George Peele's Biblical Drama," *ES*, 39 (1958): 57-62.

476. Greg, W. W. *Two Elizabethan Stage Abridgements: the Battle of Alcazar and Orlando Furioso. An Essay in Critical Bibliography*. Oxford, 1923.

477. Hook, F. "The Two Compositors in the First Quarto of Peele's *Edward I*," SB, 7 (1955): 170-171.

478. *Prouty, C. T., gen. ed. *The Life and Works of George Peele*. 3 vols. New Haven, 1952-70.

479: Ribner, I. "Shakespeare and Peele: the Death of Cleopatra," *N&Q*, 197 (1952): 244-246.

480. Rice, W. G. "A Principle Source of the *Battle of Alcazar*," *MLN*, 58 (1943): 428-431.

481. Sampley, A. M. "The Text of Peele's *David and Bethsabe*," *PMLA*, 46 (1931): 659-671.

482. Sampley, A. M. "The Version of the Bible Used by Peele in the Composition of *David and Bethsabe*," *Studies in English, University of Texas*, 8 (1928): 78-87.

See also 699, 718, 720.

ANON.

King Leir and His Three Daughters (c. 1590)

483. Crundell, H. W. "Anthony Mundy and *King Leir*," *N&Q*, 166 (1934): 310-311.

484. Elton, W. R. *"King Lear" and the Gods,* San Marino, Calif., 1966, pp. 63-71, and *passim.*

485. *Greg, W. W., ed. *King Leir.* London, 1908.

486. Law, R. A. "Holinshed's Leir Story and Shakespeare's," *SP,* 47 (1950): 42-50.

487. Wells, W. "The Authorship of *King Leir," N&Q,* 177 (1939): 434-438.

ANON.

Life and Death of Jacke Straw (1591)

488. Adkins, M. G. M. "A Theory about the *Life and Death of Jack Straw," Studies in English, University of Texas,* 28 (1949): 57-82.

489. *Muir, K., ed. *Life and Death of Jack Straw.* London, 1957.

See also 699.

ANON.

Lamentable Tragedy of Locrine (c. 1591)

490. Bald, R. C. "The *Locrine* and *George-a-Greene* Title-page Inscriptions," *Library,* 15 (1934): 295-305.

491. E. K. B. *"Locrine* and the *Faerie Queene," The Nation,* 107 (1918): 296.

492. Farnham, W. "John Higgins' *Mirror* and *Locrine," MP,* 23 (1926): 307-313.

493. Graves, T. S. "The Authorship of *Locrine," TLS,* January 8, 1925, p. 24.

494. *McKerrow, R. B., ed. *Locrine.* London, 1908.

495. Muir, K. *"Locrine* and *Selimus," TLS,* August 12, 1944, p. 391.

See also 242, 686, 699, 718.

ANON.

Lamentable and True Tragedy of Master Arden of Fever-sham (c. 1592)

496. Adams, H. H. *English Domestic or Homiletic Tragedy, 1575-1642. Being an Account of the Development of the Tragedy of the Common Man, Showing its Great Dependence on Religious Morality, Illustrated with Striking Examples of the Interposition of Providence for the Amendment of Men's Manners*. Columbia University Studies in English and Comparative Literature, no. 159. New York, 1943.

497. Blayney, G. H. *"Arden of Feversham*—An Early Reference," *N&Q*, 2 (1955): 336.

498. Bluestone, M. "The Imagery of Tragic Melodrama in *Arden of Feversham," DramS*, 5 (1966): 171-181.

499. Chapman R. *"Arden of Feversham*: Its Interest Today," *English*, 11 (1956): 15-17.

500. Cornelius, R. D. "Mosbie's 'Stary Gaile'," *PQ*, 9 (1930): 70-72; 394-396.

501. Gillet, L. *"Arden de Feversham,"* in *Le Théâtre elizabéthain*, Cahiers du Sud. X Numéro Spécial (1933): 154-161.

502. Greg, W. W. *"Arden of Faversham," TLS*, January 24, 1924, p. 53.

503. Grubb, M. "A Brace of Villains," *MLN*, 50 (1935): 168-169.

504. Jackson, M. P. "An Emendation to *Arden of Feversham," N&Q*, 10 (1963): 410.

505. Lawrence, W. J. "The Authorship of *Arden of Feversham," TLS*, June 28, 1934, p. 460.

506. *Macdonald, H. and D. N. Smith, eds. *Arden of Feversham*. London, 1940 (1947).

507. Montaigne, A. *"Arden de Feversham*, adapte par H. R. Lenormand," *Le Mois*, October, 1938, pp. 226-228.

508. Nosworthy, J. M. "The Southouse Text of *Arden of Feversham," Library*, 5 (1950): 113-129.

509. Oliphant, E. H. C. *"Arden of Feversham," TLS*, January 18, 1936, p. 55.

510. Oliphant, E. H. C. "Marlowe's Hand in *Arden of Feversham," New Criterion*, 4 (1926): 76-93.

511. Tannenbaum, S. A. "Mosbie's 'Stary Gaile' Again," *PQ*, 9 (1930): 213-215.

512. Taylor, E. A. "Elizabethan Domestic Tragedies," Ph.D. Thesis. U. of Chicago, 1928.

513. Wentersdorf, K. P. "The 'Fence of Trouble' Crux in *Arden of Faversham?" N&Q,* 4 (1957): 160-161.

514. Wolff, M. J. "Zu *Arden von Feversham," Die Neueren Sprachen,* 35 (1927): 424-427.

515. Youngblood, S. "Theme and Imagery in *Arden of Feversham," SEL,* 3 (1963): 207-218.

See also 348, 516, 699.

ANON.

True Tragedie of Richard the Third (1588-1594)

516. Crundell, H. W. *"Arden* and *Richard III," N&Q,* 166 (1934): 456-458.

517. *Greg, W. W., ed. *True Tragedy of Richard III, 1594.* Oxford and London, 1929.

518. Mott, L. F. "Foreign Politics in an Old Play," *MP,* 19 (1921): 65-71.

519. Zeeveld, W. "A Tudor Defense of Richard III," *PMLA,* 55 (1940): 956-957.

See also 496, 599, 699, 720, 734.

SAMUEL DANIEL

Cleopatra (1594)

Philotas (c. 1600)

520. Blissett, W. "Samuel Daniel's Sense of the Past," *ES,* 38 (1957): 49-63.

521. Brady, G. K. "Samuel Daniel: a Critical Study," Ph.D. Thesis. U. of Illinois, 1926.

522. Drewey, C. H. "Samuel Daniel's *Tragedy of Philotas:* the Use of Contradiction and Paradox as Methods of Comment upon the Essex Affair and Upon the Responsibilities of Monarchs," *DA,* 28 (1967): 2365-A (Northwestern).

523. Godshalk, W. L. "Daniel's *History," JEGP,* 63 (1964): 45-57.

524. Himelick, R. "Samuel Daniel, Montaigne and Seneca," *N&Q,* 3 (1956): 61-64.

525. Leavenworth, R. E. "Daniel's *Cleopatra:* a Critical Study," Ph.D. Thesis. U. of Colorado, 1954.

526. *Michel, L. "An Edition of Samuel Daniel's *Philotas* with Introduction and Notes," Ph.D. Thesis. Fordham University, 1943.

527. Michel, L. and C. C. Seronsy. "Shakespeare's History Plays and Daniel: an Assessment," *SP,* 52 (1955): 549-577.

528. *Michel, L., ed. *The Tragedy of Philotas by Samuel Daniel, YSE,* no. 110. New Haven, 1949.

529. Norgaard, H. "The Bleeding Captain Scene in *Macbeth* and Daniel's *Cleopatra,*" *RES,* 6 (1955): 395-396.

530. Norman, A. "Daniel's the *Tragedie of Cleopatra* and *Antony and Cleopatra,*" *SQ,* 9 (1958): 11-18.

531. Norman, A. "The *Tragedie of Cleopatra* and the Date of *Antony and Cleopatra,*" *MLR,* 54 (1959): 1-9.

532. Rees, J. "Samuel Daniel's *Cleopatra* and Two French Plays," *MLR,* 47 (1952): 1-10.

533. *Sampson, H., ed. "A Critical Edition of Samuel Daniel's the *Tragedie of Cleopatra,*" *DA,* 27 (1966): 3017-A (St. Louis).

534. Schanzer, E. "Daniel's Revision of his *Cleopatra,*" *RES,* 8 (1957): 375-381 (reply J. Rees, *RES,* 9 (1958): 294-295).

535. Schütze, J. "Daniel's *Cleopatra* and Shakespeare," *EStudien,* 71 (1936): 58-72.

536. Seronsy, C. C. "The Doctrine of Cyclical Recurrence and Some Related Ideas in the Works of Samuel Daniel," *SP,* 54 (1957): 387-407.

537. Stirling, B. "Cleopatra's Scene with Seleucus: Plutarch, Daniel, and Shakespeare," *SQ,* 15 (1964): 299-311.

538. Stirling, B. "Daniel's *Philotas* and the Essex Case," *MLQ,* 3 (1942): 583-594.

539. Uhland, M. "A Study of Samuel Daniel," Ph.D. Thesis. Cornell, 1937.

540. Wilkes, G. "Daniel's *Philotas* and the Essex Case: a Reconsideration," *MLQ,* 23 (1962): 233-242.

See also 286, 290, 570.

GEORGE CHAPMAN

Bussy D'Ambois (1596-1604)

541. Barber, C. L. "The Ambivalence of *Bussy D'Ambois*," *REL*, 2, iv (1961): 38-44.

542. Battenhouse, R. W. "Chapman and the Nature of Man," *ELH*, 12 (1945): 87-107.

543. Burton, K. M. "The Political Tragedies of Chapman and Ben Jonson," *EIC*, 2 (1952): 397-412.

544. Cole, G. W. "Bibliographical Ghosts: *Bussy D'Ambois* by George Chapman; *Of the Circumference of the Earth* by Dudley Digges; *The Bloody Banquet* by T. D.," *PBSA*, 13 (1919): 87-112.

545. Crawley, D. "Character in Relation to Action in the Tragedies of George Chapman," *DA*, 24 (1963): 3728 (Northwestern).

546. Engel, C-E. "Les sources du *Bussy D'Ambois* de Chapman," *RLC*, 12 (1932): 587-595.

547. Freehafer, J. "The Contention for *Bussy D'Ambois*, 1622-41," *TN*, 23 (1968/69): 61-69.

548. Haddakin, L. "A Note on Chapman and Two Medieval English Jurists," *MLR*, 47 (1952): 550-553.

549. Hibbard, G. R. "Goodness and Greatness: an Essay on the Tragedies of Ben Jonson and George Chapman," *RMS*, 2 (1968): 5-54.

550. Higgins, M. "The Development of the 'Senecal Man': Chapman's *Bussy D'Ambois* and Some Precursors," *RES*, 23 (1947): 24-33.

551. Howarth, R. G. "The Date of *Bussy D'Ambois*," *N&Q*, 177 (1939): 25.

552. Jacquot, J. "*Bussy D'Ambois* and Chapman's Conception of Tragedy," in *English Studies Today*, ed. by S. Bonnard. Bern, 1961, pp. 129-141.

553. Kandaswami, S. "Chapman's *Bussy D'Ambois:* a Metaphysical Drama," *Mother India*, 12 (1960): 55-58.

554. Leech, C. "The *Atheist's Tragedy* as a Dramatic Comment on Chapman's *Bussy* Plays," *JEGP*, 52 (1953): 525-530.

555. Loane, G. G. "Bussy D'Ambois' Dying Words," *TLS,* March 1, 1923, p. 143.

556. McCollom, W. G. "The Tragic Hero and Chapman's *Bussy D'Ambois,*" *UTQ,* 18 (1949): 227-233.

557. Meyers, R. "The Royal King and Loyal Subject: Changing Political Conceptions Reflected in the Drama of Beaumont, Fletcher and Chapman." Ph.D. Thesis. New York University, 1964.

558. Muir, E. " 'Royal Man' Notes on the Tragedies of George Chapman, *Orion,* ed. by R. Lehmann and others. Vol. 2. London, 1945, pp. 92-100.

559. Ornstein, R. "The Date of Chapman's Tragedies, Once More," *MP,* 59 (1961): 61-64.

560. *Parrott, T. M., ed. *The Tragedies of George Chapman.* 2 vols. New York, 1961.

561. Perkinson, R. H. "Nature and the Tragic Hero in Chapman's *Bussy* Plays," *MLQ,* 3, (1942): 263-285.

562. Rees, E. *The Tragedies of George Chapman: Renaissance Ethics in Action.* Cambridge, Mass., 1954.

563. Reese, J. "The 'Circular' Man: a Study of Chapman's Heroes." Ph.D. Thesis. U. of Kentucky, 1962.

564. Ribner, I. "Character and Theme in Chapman's *Bussy D'Ambois,*" *ELH,* 26 (1959): 482-496.

565. Schrickx, W. "Mythological Patterns in Chapman's *Bussy D'Ambois:* Their Interpretive Value," *RLV,* 18 (1952): 279-286.

566. Schwartz, E. "Seneca, Homer, and Chapman's *Bussy D'Ambois,*" *JEGP,* 56 (1957): 163-176.

567. Schwartz, E. "The Dates and Order of Chapman's Tragedies," *MP,* 57 (1959): 80-82.

568. Schwartz, E. "The Date of *Bussy D'Ambois,*" *MP,* 59 (1961): 126-127.

569. Sturman, B. "The 1641 Edition of Chapman's *Bussy D'Ambois,*" *HLQ,* 14 (1951): 171-201.

570. Ure, P. "A Note on 'Opinion' in Daniel, Greville, and Chapman," *MLR,* 46 (1951): 331-338.

571. Ure, P. "Chapman's Tragedies," in *Jacobean Theatre*, ed. by J. Brown and B. Harris. London, 1960, pp. 227-247.

572. Ure, P. "Chapman's Tragedy of *Bussy D'Ambois:* Problems of the Revised Quarto," *MLR*, 48 (1953): 257-269.

573. Ure, P. "The Date of the Revision of Chapman's the *Tragedy of Bussy D'Ambois*," *N&Q*, 197 (1952): 1-2.

574. Waddington, R. B. "Prometheus and Hercules: the Dialectic of *Bussy D'Ambois*," *ELH*, 34 (1967): 21-48.

575. Weiss, A. B. "Chapman's *Bussy D'Ambois*, Act III, Scene iii," *Expl*, 27 (1969): Item 56.

576. Wieler, J. W. *George Chapman—The Effect of Stoicism upon His Tragedies*. New York, 1949.

See also 650, 686, 718, 720, 730, 737, 739, 743.

ROBERT GREENE

The First Part of the Tragicall Raigne of Selimus (1586-1593)

577. *Brooke, C. F. T., ed. *Selimus,* in *The Shakespeare Apocrypha*. Oxford, 1908.

578. Ekeblad, I-S. *"King Lear and Selimus,"* N&Q, 4 (1957): 193-195.

579. Freeman, A. "An Unacknowledged Work of Robert Greene," *N&Q*, 12 (1965): 378-379.

580. Jacquot, J. "A propos du *Tragicall Raigne of Selimus:* Le problème des emprunts aux classiques à la renaissance," *EA*, 16 (1963): 345-350.

581. Jacquot, J. "Ralegh's 'Hellish Verses' and the *Tragicall Raigne of Selimus*," *MLR*, 48 (1953): 1-9.

582. Jacquot, J. *"The Tragicall Raigne of Selimus et la conception elisabethaine de l'athee,"* EA, 7 (1954): 199-205.

583. Muir, K. "Greene and *Troilus and Cressida*," *N&Q*, 2 (1955): 141-142.

584. Ribner, I. "Greene's Attack on Marlowe: Some Light on *Alphonsus* and *Selimus*," *SP*, 52 (1955): 162-171.

585. Sanders, N. "Robert Greene's Way with a Source," *N&Q*, 14 (1967): 89-91.

See also 495, 718.

RICHARD FARRANT

Warres of Cyrus King of Persia (1587-1594)

586. *Brawner, J. P., ed. *The Wars of Cyrus, an Early Classical Narrative Drama of the Child Actors:* Critical Edition with Introduction and Notes. Urbana, 1945.

587. Hunter, G. K. "The *Wars of Cyrus* and *Tamburlaine,*" *N&Q,* 8 (1961): 395-396.

588. Ribner, I. *"Tamburlaine* and the *Wars of Cyrus,"* *JEGP,* 53 (1954): 569-573.

See also 699.

ROBERT YARRINGTON

Two Lamentable Tragedies (c. 1594)

589. *Bullen, A. H., ed. *Two Lamentable Tragedies,* in *A Collection of Old English Plays.* 4 vols. New York, 1964.

590. Cawley, A. C. *"A Yorkshire Tragedy* and *Two Most Vnnatural and Bloodie Murthers,"* in *The Morality of Art: Essays Presented to G. Wilson Knight by His Colleagues and Friends,* ed. by D. W. Jefferson. London, 1969, pp. 102-118.

591. Golding, S. R. "The Authorship of the *Two Lamentable Tragedies,"* *N&Q,* 151 (1926): 347-350.

592. Law, R. A. "Further Notes on *Two Lamentable Tragedies,"* *N&Q,* 153 (1927): 93-94.

593. Wagner, B. M. "Robert Yarrington," *MLN,* 45 (1930): 147-148.

See also 496.

B. J. (Possibly DEKKER)

Tragical History of Guy of Warwick (1592-1639)

594. *Bowers, F. T., ed. *The Dramatic Works of Thomas Dekker.* 4 vols. Cambridge, 1961.

595. Greg, W. W. *"Guy of Warwick,"* *MLR,* 19 (1924): 337-338.

ANON.

Woodstock, or Thomas Duke of Glocester (1591-1595)

596. Lloyd, B. "Jonson and *Thomas of Woodstock,"* *TLS,* July 17, 1924, p. 449.

597. *Rossiter, A. P., ed. *I Richard II, Woodstock,* or *Thomas Duke of Glocester.* London, 1946.

ANON.

Sir Thomas More (c. 1596)

598. Bald, R. C. "Addition III of *Sir Thomas More,*" *RES,* 7 (1931): 67-69.

599. Chambers, R. W. "Some Sequences of Thought in Shakespeare and in the 147 Lines of *Sir Thomas More,*" *MLR,* 26 (1931): 251-280.

600. Collins, D. C. "On the Date of *Sir Thomas More,*" *RES,* 10 (1934): 401-411 (see also *N&Q,* 167 (1934): 271, and H. W. Crundell, "Shakespeare and Essex," *N&Q,* 167 (1934): 316-317).

601. Golding, S. R. "Robert Wilson and *Sir Thomas More,*" *N&Q,* 154 (1928): 237-239, 259-262; also in 155 (1929): 237-240.

602. *Greg, W. W., ed. *Sir Thomas More.* London, 1911.

603. Harrison, G. "The Date of *Sir Thomas More,*" *RES,* 1 (1925): 468-469.

604. Jackson, M. "Anthony Mundy and *Sir Thomas More,*" *N&Q,* 10 (1963): 96.

605. Law, R. A. "Is Heywood's Hand in *Sir Thomas More?*" *Studies in English, University of Texas,* no. 11 (1932): 24-31.

606. Marschall, W. "Das *Sir Thomas More*—Manuskript und die Englishche *Commedia Dell'Arte,*" *Anglia,* 52 (1928): 193-241.

607. Oliphant, E. H. C. "The Shakespeare Canon," *QR,* 259 (1932): 32-48.

608. Pollard, A. W. and J. D. Wilson. *Shakespeare's Hand in the Play of Sir Thomas More.* Papers by A. W. Pollard, W. W. Greg, E. M. Thompson, J. D. Wilson, and R. W. Chambers with a text of the III May Day Scenes edited by W. W. Greg. Cambridge, 1923.

609. Pollard, A. W. "The Date of the Play of *Sir Thomas More,*" *TLS,* Nov. 8, 1923, p. 751.

610. Schütt, M. "Die Quellen des *Book of Sir Thomas More*," *EStudien,* 68 (1933): 209-226.

611. Spurgeon, C. F. E. "Imagery in the *Sir Thomas More* Fragment," *RES,* 6 (1930): 257-270.

612. Tannenbaum, S. A. *The Booke of Sir Thomas More.* New York, 1927.

613. Tannenbaum, S. A. "More about the *Booke of Sir Thomas More,*" *PMLA,* 43 (1929): 767-778 (reply by W. W. Greg, 44 (1929): 633-634; rejoinder by Tannenbaum, 44 (1929): 934-938; correction by Greg, 44 (1929): 938; and another volley by Greg, 46 (1931): 268-271).

See also 496, 678, 699.

FULKE GREVILLE

Mustapha (c. 1596)

Alaham (1598-1600)

614. *Bullough, G., ed. *The Poems and Dramas of Fulke Greville.* 2 vols. Edinburgh, 1939.

615. Carter, B. "The Intellectual Background of Fulke Greville," *DA,* 15 (1955): 1061-1062 (Stanford).

616. Edwards, D. C. "Fulke Greville on Tragedy," *TLS,* June 8, 1940, p. 279.

617. Maclean, H. N. "Bacon, Greville, History and Biography," *N&Q,* 3 (1956): 95-97.

618. Maclean, H. N. "Fulke Greville and 'E. K.'," *ELN,* 1 (1963): 90-100.

619. Maclean, H. N. "Fulke Greville: Kingship and Sovereignty," *HLQ,* 16 (1953): 237-271.

620. Mahoney, J. F. "Donne and Greville: Two Christian Attitudes Toward the Renaissance Idea of Mutability and Decay," *CLAJ,* 5 (1962): 203-212.

621. Morris, I. "The Tragic Vision of Fulke Greville," *ShS,* 14 (1961): 66-75.

622. Newman, F. B. "Sir Fulke Greville and Giordano Bruno: a Possible Echo," *PQ,* 29 (1950): 367-374.

623. Oras, A. "Fulke Greville's *Mustapha* and Robert Wilmot's *Tancred and Gismund,*" *N&Q,* 7 (1960): 24-25.

624. Rice, W. G. "The Sources of Fulke Greville's *Alaham*," *JEGP*, 30 (1931): 179-187.

625. Thaler, A. "Franklin and Fulke Greville," *PMLA*, 56 (1941): 1059-1064.

626. Ure, P. "Fulke Greville's Dramatic Characters," *RES*, 1 (1950): 308-323.

627. Wilkes, G. "The Sequence of the Writings of Fulke Greville, Lord Brooke," *SP*, 56 (1959): 489-503.

628. Wilkes, G. "The Sources of Fulke Greville's *Mustapha*," *N&Q*, 5 (1958): 329-330.

See also 570, 718, 749.

HENRY CHETTLE

The Tragedy of Hoffman (c. 1598)

The Death of Robert Earl of Huntington (with Munday, 1598)

629. Byrne, M. St. C. "Bibliographical Clues in Collaborate Plays," *Library*, 13 (1932): 21-48.

630. Jenkins, H. "The 1631 Quarto of the *Tragedy of Hoffman*," *Library*, 6 (1951): 88-99.

631. *Jenkins, H., ed. *Tragedy of Hoffman, 1631*. Oxford, 1951.

632. Schlochauer, E. J. "A Note on Variants in the Dedication of Chettle's *Tragedy of Hoffman*," *PBSA*, 42 (1948): 307-312.

633. Thomas, S. "Henry Chettle and the First Quarto of *Romeo and Juliet*," *RES*, 1 (1950): 8-16.

See also 636, 642, 686, 720.

ANTHONY MUNDAY

The Downfall of Robert Earl of Huntington (1598)

The Death of Robert Earl of Huntington (with Chettle, 1958)

634. Byrne, M. St. C. "Anthony Munday and His Books," *Library*, 4 (March, 1921): 225-256.

635. Byrne, M. St. C. "Anthony Munday's Spelling as a Literary Clue," *Library*, 4, (1923): 9-23.

636. *Farmer, J. S., ed. *Downfall of Robert Earl of Huntington* and *Death of Robert Earl of Huntington,* in *Old English Plays, Student's Facsimile Edition.* Amersham, England, 1913, vols. 15, 16.

637. McPeek, J. A. S. *"Macbeth* and Mundy Again," *MLN,* 46 (1931): 391-392.

638. *Pittman, G. C. "A Critical Edition of Anthony Munday's the *Downfall of Robert, Earl of Huntington,"* *DA,* 28 (1968): 3154A (Mississippi).

639. Shapiro, I. A. "Shakespeare and Munday," *ShS,* 14 (1961): 25-33.

640. Turner, C. *Anthony Munday, An Elizabethan Man of Letters. University of California Publications in English,* Vol. II, no. 1 (1928): 1-234.

641. Wright, C. T. "Anthony Mundy 'Edward' Spenser, and E. K.," *PMLA,* 76 (1961): 34-39.

642. Wright, C. T. "Mundy and Chettle in Grub Street," *BUSE,* 5 (1961): 129-138.

643. Wright, C. T. "Young Anthony Munday Again," *SP,* 56 (1959): 150-168.

See also 483, 604, 629, 720.

THOMAS HEYWOOD

A Warning for Fair Women (c. 1588-1599)

644. Cannon, C. K. *"A Warning for Fair Women:* a Critical Edition," *DA,* 25 (1964): 1889-1890 (U. of Mississippi).

645. Cohen, D. *"A Warning for Fair Women,"* Ph.D. Thesis. Radcliff, 1957.

646. Lewis, A. C., Jr. *"A Warning for Faire Women* (Line 143)," *N&Q,* 1 (1954): 18-19.

647. Martin, R. G. "A New Specimen of the Revenge Play," *MP,* 16 (1918-1919): 1-10.

See also 605, 730.

JOHN MARSTON

Antonio's Revenge (1599-1601)

648. Allen, M. S. *The Satire of John Marston.* New York, 1965, pp. 128-134.

649. Atkins, S. "Marston and Everard Guilpin," *TLS,* June 9, 1932, p. 427.

650. Bergson, A. "A Study of the Ironic Tragedies of Marston and Chapman," *DA,* 29, (1968): 1223-A (U. of California, Berkeley).

651. Caputi, A. *John Marston, Satirist.* Ithaca, New York, 1961, pp. 117-157, and *passim.*

652. Eliot, T. S. "John Marston," in *Essays on Elizabethan Drama.* New York, 1956, pp. 162-178.

653. Floyd, J. P. "The Convention of Melancholy in the Plays of Marston and Shakespeare." Ph.D. Thesis. Harvard, 1942.

654. Foakes, R. "John Marston's Fantastical Plays: *Antonio and Mellida* and *Antonio's Revenge,*" *PQ,* 41 (1962): 229-239.

655. Forker, C. R. "Tennyson's 'Tithonous' and Marston's *Antonio's Revenge,*" *N&Q,* 6 (1959): 445.

656. Higgins, M. "The Convention of the Stoic Hero as Handled by Marston," *MLR,* 39 (1944): 338-346.

657. *Hunter, G. K., ed. *Antonio's Revenge.* Lincoln, 1965, pp. ix-xxi.

658. Hunter, G. K. "English Folly and Italian Vice: the Moral Landscape of John Marston," in *Jacobean Theatre,* ed. J. R. Brown and B. Harris. Stratford-upon-Avon Studies, no. 1. London, 1960, pp. 85-111.

659. Hunter, G. K. "The Spoken Dirge in Kyd, Marston [*Antonio's Revenge,* IV, ii. 88ff] and Shakespeare: a Background to *Cymbeline,*" *N&Q,* 11 (1964): 146-147.

660. McGinn, D. J. "A New Date for *Antonio's Revenge,*" *PMLA,* 53 (1938): 129-137.

661. Peter, J. "John Marston's Plays," *Scrutiny,* 17 (1950): 132-153.

662. Peter, J. "Marston's Use of Seneca," *N&Q,* 1 (1954): 145-149.

663. Prosser, E. *Hamlet and Revenge.* Stanford, Calif., 1967, pp. 57-62 and *passim.*

664. Spencer, T. "John Marston," *New Criterion,* 13 (1934): 581-599.

665. *Wood, H. H., ed. *Plays of John Marston, Volume I.* Edinburgh, 1934.

See also 449, 686, 728, 737, 739.

JOHN DAY (with DEKKER AND HAUGHTON)

Lust's Dominion (1600)

666. Brereton, J. L., ed. *Lust's Dominion.* Materials for the Study of the Old English Drama. Louvain, 1931.

667. Cross, G. "The Authorship of *Lust's Dominian,*" SP, 55 (1958): 39-61.

668. Cross, G. "More's *Historie of Kyng Rycharde the Thirde* and *Lust's Dominion,*" N&Q, 4 (1957): 198-199.

669. Schoenbaum, S. "John Day and Elizabethan Drama," *BPLQ,* 5 (1953): 140-152.

See also 686, 720.

III. GENERAL AND MISCELLANEOUS STUDIES

III. GENERAL AND MISCELLANEOUS STUDIES

A. General

670. Adams, C. N. "The Role of Anxiety in English Tragedy: 1580-1642," *DA,* 28 (1967): 2198-A (S. Carolina).

671. Aggeler, G. D. "The Ethical Problems of Revenge in English Renaissance Tragedy," *DA,* 27 (1967): 3830-A (U. of California, Davis, 1966).

672. Anderson, R. L. "Excessive Goodness a Tragic Fault," *SAB,* 19 (1944): 85-96.

673. Anderson, R. L. "The Mirror Concept and its Relation to the Drama of the Renaissance," *Northwest Mississippi State Teacher's College Studies,* 3 (1939): 1-30.

674. Armstrong, W. A. "The Elizabethan Conception of the Tyrant," *RES,* 22 (1946): 161-181.

675. Babb, L. "Melancholic Villainy in the Elizabethan Drama," *PMASAL,* 29 (1943): 527-535.

676. Bemrose, J. M. "A Critical Examination of the Borrowings from *Venus and Adonis* and *Lucrece* in Samuel Nicholson's *Acolastus,*" *SQ,* 15 (1964): 85-96.

677. Bevan, E. "Revenge, Forgiveness, and the Gentleman," *REL,* 8 (1967): 55-69.

678. Bevington, D. M. *From "Mankind" to Marlowe.* Cambridge, Mass., 1962, *passim.*

679. Bevington, D. M. *Tudor Drama and Politics: a Critical Approach to Topical Meaning.* Cambridge, Mass., 1968, *passim.*

680. Blissett, W. "Lucan's Caesar and the Elizabethan Villain," *SP,* 53 (1956): 553-575.

681. Bolen, F. E. "Irony and Self-Knowledge in the Creation of Tragedy," *DA,* 25 (1964): 449-450 (U. of Mississippi, 1963).

682. Bonjour, A. "The Test of Poetry," *ShJB,* 100 (1964): 149-158.

683. Boughner, D. "Retribution in English Medieval Drama," *N&Q,* 198 (1953): 506-508.

684. Bowers, F. T. "The Audience and the Poisoners of Elizabethan Tragedy," *JEGP,* 36 (1937): 491-504.

685. Bowers, F. T. "The Audience and the Revenger of Elizabethan Tragedy," *SP,* 31 (1934): 160-175.

686. Bowers, F. T. *Elizabethan Revenge Tragedy, 1587-1642.* Princeton, 1940.

687. Bowers, F. T. "The Stabbing of a Portrait in Elizabethan Tragedy," *MLN,* 47 (1932): 378-385.

688. Bowers, R. H. "A Middle English Wheel of Fortune Poem," *ES,* 41 (1960): 196-198.

689. Caldwell, H. B. "The Child Tragic Ballad: a Comparison with Medieval Literary Tragedy—Boccaccio, Chaucer, Lydgate," *DA,* 29 (1968): 865A (Vanderbilt).

690. Campbell, L. B. *Shakespeare's Tragic Heroes: Slaves of Passion.* New York, 1958 (Cambridge, 1930), pp. 3-24.

691. Campbell, L. B. "Theories of Revenge in Renaissance England," *MP,* 28 (1931): 281-296.

692. Clark, D. L. "Ancient Rhetoric and English Renaissance Literature," *SQ,* 2 (1951): 195-204.

693. Cole, D. "The Comic Accomplice in Elizabethan Revenge Tragedy," *RenD,* 9 (1966): 125-139.

694. Craig, H. "The Shackling of Accidents: a Study of Elizabethan Tragedy," *PQ,* 19 (1940): 1-19.

695. De Chickera, E. B. "Palaces of Pleasure: the Theme of Revenge in Elizabethan Translations of Novelle," *RES,* 11 (1960): 1-7.

696. Dent, R. W. " 'Quality of Insight' in Elizabethan and Jacobean Tragedy," *MP,* 63 (1966): 252-256.

697. Doran, M. *Endeavors of Art: a Study of Form in Elizabethan Drama.* Madison, 1954, *passim.*

698. Durfee, J. "A Study of Expectation and Surprise in Tragedy, Especially Elizabethan and Jacobean." Ph.D. Thesis. U. of Colorado, 1941.

699. Farnham, W. *The Medieval Heritage of Elizabethan Tragedy.* Oxford, 1963 (1936), pp. 69-136, 160-478.

700. Fryxell, B. L. "Ghosts and Witches in Elizabethan Tragedy." Ph.D. Thesis. U. of Wisconsin, 1938.

701. Gatto, L. C. "Suicide and Utopian Philosophy," *BSUF,* 9 (1968): 33-38.

702. Graves, T. S. "The Comedy of Stage Death," *SAQ,* 21 (1922): 109-126.

703. Harbage, A. "Intrigue in Elizabethan Tragedy," in *Essays on Shakespeare and the Elizabethan Drama in honor of Hardin Craig, ed. by R. Hosley.* Columbia, 1962, pp. 37-44.

704. Harmon, A. I. "Loci Communes on Death and Suicide in the Literature of the English Renaissance." Ph.D. Thesis. U. of Minnesota, 1949.

705. Harrison, F. "Greek and Elizabethan Tragedy," *The Nineteenth Century and After,* 85 (1919): 685-699.

706. Herndl, G. C. "Changing Conceptions of Natural Law in the Jacobean Period: the Philosophical Origins of the Decline of Tragedy," *DA,* 26 (1966): 3923-3924 (U. of North Carolina, 1965).

707. Herrick, M. T. *Italian Tragedy in the Renaissance.* Urbana, 1965.

708. Hicks, C. E. "Suicide in English Tragedy, 1587-1622," *DA,* 29 (1968): 1868-A-1869-A (U. of Texas).

709. Iwatsuki, T. "On the Changing Literary Modes in the Development of Renaissance Tragedy," *SELit,* 18 (1938): 486-505.

710. Johnson, S. F. "The Tragic Hero in Early Elizabethan Drama," in *Studies in the English Renaissance Drama: In Memory of Karl Julius Holzknecht,* ed. by J. W. Bennett, O. Cargill, and V. Hall, Jr. New York, 1959, pp. 157-171.

711. Leech, C. "The Implications of Tragedy," *English,* 6 (1947): 177-182.

712. Lewis, C. S. *The Discarded Image: an Introduction to Medieval and Renaissance Literature.* Cambridge, 1964, pp. 75-91.

713. Littlefield, R. L. "Knowledge, Opinion, and Tragedy: a Survey from Mythic Origins to Elizabethan Tragedy," *DA,* 26 (1966): 5414 (Texas Tech.).

714. Long, R. A. "John Heywood, Chaucer, and Lydgate," *MLN,* 64 (1949): 55-56.

715. McCollom, W. G. "Illusion and Formalism in Elizabethan Tragedy." Ph.D. Thesis. Cornell, 1944.

716. McCullen, J. T. "Madness and Isolation of Character in Elizabethan and Early Stuart Drama," *SP,* 48 (1951): 206-218.

717. McDonald, C. O. *"Decorum, Ethos,* and *Pathos* in the Heroes of Elizabethan Tragedy, with Particular Reference to *Hamlet," JEGP,* 61 (1962): 339-348.

718. McDonald, C. O. *The Rhetoric of Tragedy: Form in Stuart Drama.* Amherst, Mass., 1966.

719. McIntyre, C. F. "The Later Career of the Elizabethan Villain-Hero," *PMLA,* 40 (1925): 874-880.

720. Margeson, J. M. R. *The Origins of English Tragedy.* Oxford, 1967.

721. Mason, E. C. "Satire on Women and Sex in Elizabethan Tragedy," *ES,* 31 (1950): 1-10.

722. Mincoff, M. "Verbal Repetition in Elizabethan Tragedy," *God.,* 41 (1945): 1-128.

723. Nicoll, A. " 'Tragical—Comical—Historical—Pastoral': Elizabethan Dramatic Nomenclature," *BJRL,* 43 (1960): 12-45.

724. Ornstein, R. *The Moral Vision of Jacobean Tragedy.* Madison, 1960.

725. Palmer, D. J. "Elizabethan Tragic Heroes," in *Elizabethan Theatre,* ed. by J. R. Brown and B. Harris. Stratford-upon-Avon Studies, no. 9. London, 1966, pp. 11-35.

726. Powell, A. F. "The Melting Mood: a Study of the Function of Pathos in English Tragedy through Shakespeare." Ph.D. Thesis. Vanderbilt, 1949.

727. Prasad, P. "The Order of Complaint: a Study in the Medieval Tradition," *DA,* 26 (1966): 3930 (U. of Wisconsin).

728. Praz, M. "Machiavelli and the Elizabethans," *PBA,* 14 (1928): 49-97 (reprinted in *The Flaming Heart,* New York, 1958, pp. 90-145).

729. Praz, M. *Teatro elisabettiano: Kyd-Marlowe-Heywood-Marston-Johnson-Webster-Tourneur-Ford.* Firenze, 1948.

730. Ribner, I. *Jacobean Tragedy. The Quest for Moral Order.* New York and London, 1962.

731. Saner, R. "Romeo and Juliet in Sixteenth-Century Drama," *DA,* 23 (1962): 626 (U. of Illinois).

732. Sasayama, T. "The Tragic Vision and the Problem of Revenge: an Essay on the Nature of the Elizabethan Tragedy," *SELit,* 38 (1961): 187-200.

733. Saunders, T. "Religion and Tragedy," *DR,* 24 (1944): 283-297.

734. Schuster, M. F. "Philosophy of Life and Prose Style in Thomas More's *Richard III* and Francis Bacon's *Henry VII,*" *PMLA,* 70 (1955): 474-487.

735. Sibly, J. "The Duty of Revenge in Tudor and Stuart Drama," *REL,* 8 (1967): 46-54.

736. Simpson, P. "The Theme of Revenge in Elizabethan Tragedy," Annual Shakespeare Lecture of the British Academy, 1935. Oxford, 1935.

737. Stagg, L. C. "An Analysis and Comparison of the Imagery in the Tragedies of Chapman, Heywood, Jonson, Marston, Webster, Tourneur, and Middleton," *DA,* 24 (1963): 1163-1164 (U. of Arkansas).

738. Stauffer, D. A. *English Biography before 1700.* Cambridge, Mass., 1930, pp. 52-54, 63, 126-129.

739. Stodder, J. H. "Satire in Jacobean Tragedy," *DA,* 25 (1964): 1898-1899 (U. S. C.).

740. Stroup, T. B. "The Testing Pattern in Elizabethan Tragedy," *SEL,* 3 (1963): 175-190.

741. Taylor, W. "The Villainess in Elizabethan Drama, *DA*, 17 (1957): 1756-1757 (Vanderbilt).

742. Thorp, W. "Justice in Elizabethan Tragedy," in *The Triumph of Realism in Elizabethan Drama, 1558-1612*. Princeton Studies in English, no. 3. Princeton, 1928, pp. 121-138.

743. Tomlinson, T. B. *A Study of Elizabethan and Jacobean Tragedy*. Cambridge, 1964.

744. Wilson, F. P. *The English Drama 1485-1585*, ed. G. K. Hunter. New York and Oxford, 1969, pp. 126-151.

745. Wood, G. D. "Retributive Justice: a Study of the Theme of Elizabethan Revenge Tragedy," *DA*, 24 (1963): 2466-2467 (U. of Kentucky).

B. Senecan Influence

746. Armstrong, W. A. "The Influence of Seneca and Machiavelli on the Elizabethan Tyrant," *RES*, 24 (1948): 19-35.

747. Beckingham, C. F. "Seneca's Fatalism and Elizabethan Tragedy," *MLR*, 32 (1937): 434-438.

748. Braginton, M. V. "Two Notes on Senecan Tragedy," *MLN*, 41 (1926): 468-469.

749. Bullough, G. "Sénèque, Greville and le jeune Shakespeare," in *Les tragédies de Sénèque et le théâtre de la renaissance*, ed. by J. Jacquot and M. Oddon. Paris, 1964.

750. Cohon, B. J. "Seneca's Tragedies in *Florilegia* and Elizabethan Drama," *DA*, 20 (1960): 4654 (Columbia).

751. Eidson, J. O. "Senecan Elements in Marston's *Antonio and Mellida*," *MLN*, 52 (1937): 196-197.

752. Eliot, T. S. "Seneca in Elizabethan Translation," *Essays on Elizabethan Drama*. New York, 1956, pp. 3-56.

753. Gilbert, A. H. "Seneca and the Criticism of Elizabethan Tragedy," *PQ*, 13 (1934): 370-381.

754. Hewlett, J. "The Influence of Seneca's *Epistulae Morales* on Elizabethan Tragedy." Ph.D. Thesis. U. of Chicago, 1934.

755. Hunter, G. K. "Seneca and the Elizabethans: a Case-Study in 'Influence'," *ShS*, 20 (1966): 17-26.

756. Jacquot, J. "Les tragédies de Sénèque et le théâtre elisabéthain," *EA*, 14 (1961): 343-344.

757. Palmer, R. G. Seneca's *De remediis fortuitorum and the Elizabethans:* an Essay on the Influence of Seneca's Ethical Thought in the Sixteenth Century, together with the Newly-edited Latin Text and English Translation of 1547 Entitled: Lucii Annei Senecae ad Gallioneni de Remedis Fortuitorum. The Remedyes Agaynst all Casuall Chances. Dialogus interSensum ed Rationem. A Dialogue betwene Sensualyte and Reason. Lately Translated out of Latyn into Englyshe by Robert Whyttynton Poet Laureat and Nowe Newely Imprynted Institute of Elizabethan Studies, no. 1. Chicago, 1953.

758. Small, S. A. "The Influence of Seneca," *SAB,* 10 (1935): 137-150.

759. Ure, P. "On Some Differences between Senecan and Elizabethan Tragedy," *DUJ,* 10 (1948): 17-23.

760. Wells, H. W. "Senecan Influence on Elizabethan Tragedy: a Re-Estimation," *SAB,* 19 (1944): 71-84.

See also 345, 353, 465, 471, 524, 566, 662, 751, 773.

C. Peripheral Materials

HENRY MEDWALL

Fulgens and Lucrece, I & II (1497)

761. Baskervill, C. R. "Conventional Features of Medwall's *Fulgens and Lucres,*" *MP,* 24 (1927): 419-442.

762. *Boas, F. S. and A. W. Reed, eds. *Fulgens and Lucres:* a Fifteenth Century Secular Play by Henry Medwall. Oxford, 1926.

763. Hecht, H. H. "Medwall's *Fulgens and Lucres,*" *Anglica,* Bd 2: III, 1925.

764. Jones, C. "Notes on *Fulgens and Lucrece,*" *MLN,* 50 (1935): 508-509.

765. Lowers, J. "High Comedy Elements in Medwall's *Fulgens and Lucres,*" *ELH,* 8 (1941): 103-106.

766. Reed, A. W. *Early Tudor Drama: Medwall, the Rastells, and the More Circle.* London, 1926.

767. Waith, E. *"Controversia* in the English Drama: Medwall and Massinger," *PMLA,* 68 (1953): 286-303.

768. Wright, L. B. "Notes on *Fulgens and Lucres:* New Light on the Interlude," *MLN,* 61 (1926): 97-100.

See also 678.

JOHN CHRISTOPHERSON

Jephthes (c. 1539-1544)

769. Boas, F. S. "The Tragedy of Iephte," *TLS,* Jan. 30, 1930, p. 78.

770. *Fobes, F. H., ed. *Jephthah,* introd. by W. Sypherd. Newark, 1928.

771. Wagner, B. M. "The Tragedy of Iephte," *TLS,* Dec. 26, 1929, p. 1097.

JASPER HEYWOOD
Troas, trans. of Seneca (1559)

Thyestes, trans. of Seneca (1560)

Hercules Furens, trans. of Seneca (1561)

772. *De Vocht, H., ed. *Jasper Heywood and his Translation of Seneca's Troas, Thyestes and Hercules Furens,* in *Materials for the Study of Old English Drama.* Louvain, 1913, vol. 41.

773. Greg, W. W. "Seneca's *Troas* Translated by Jasper Heywood, 1559," *Library,* 11 (1930): 162-270.

774. Pearce, T. M. "Jasper Heywood and Marlowe's *Doctor Faustus,*" *N&Q,* 197 (1952): 200-201.

ARTHUR BROOKE

The Tragicall Historye of Romeus and Juliet (1562)

775. Bodtker, A. T. "Arthur Brooke and His Poem," *EStudien,* 70 (1935): 167-168.

776. Crundell, H. W. "Arthur Brooke and *Romeo and Juliet,*" *N&Q,* 9 (1962): 205.

RICHARD EDWARDS

Damon and Pithias (c. 1565)

777. Armstrong, W. A. *"Damon and Pithias* and Renaissance Theories of Tragedy," *ES,* 39 (1958): 200-207.

778. Armstrong, W. A. "The Sources of *Damon and Pithias*," *N&Q*, 3 (1956): 146-147.

779. Bradner, L. *The Life and Poems of Richard Edwards. YSE*, no. 74. New Haven, 1927.

780. *Brown, A. and F. P. Wilson, eds. *Damon and Pythias*. London, 1957.

781. Edmonds, C. K. "No Wight in this World," *RES*, 5 (1929): 332.

782. Harvey, W. W. *"Damon and Pithias* and Other Related Plays." Ph.D. Thesis. U. of Chicago, 1929.

783. Jackson, J. L. "Three Notes on Richard Edwards' *Damon and Pythias*," *PQ*, 29 (1950): 209-213.

784. Kramer, J. E. *"Damon and Pithias:* An Apology for Art," *ELH*, 35 (1968): 475-490.

785. Mills, L. J. *Some Aspects of Richard Edwards' Damon and Pythias*. Indiana University Studies, no. 75. Bloomington, 1927.

786. Newlin, C. M. "Some Sources of Richard Edwards' *Damon and Pithias*," *MLN*, 47 (1932): 145-147.

787. Rollins, H. E. "A Note on Richard Edwards," *RES*, 5 (1929): 55-56.

See also 699.

WILLIAM GOLDING

Abraham's Sacrifice, trans. Beza (1575)

788. *Wallace, M. W., ed. *Abraham's Sacrifice*. University of Toronto Philological Series. Toronto, 1907.

789. Warren, R. "Three Notes on *A Midsummer Night's Dream*," *N&Q*, 16 (1969): 130-134.

GEORGE WHETSTONE

Promos and Cassandra (1578)

790. Amos, G. W. "A Critical Edition of George Whetstone's *Promos and Cassandra*," *DA*, 29 (1969): 3089A (U. of Arkansas).

791. Budd, F. E. "Rouillet's *Philanira* and Whetstone's *Promos and Cassandra*," *RES*, 6 (1930): 31-38.

792. *Bullough, G., ed. *Promos and Cassandra,* in *Narrative and Dramatic Sources of Shakespeare.* 6 vols. New York, 1957-66.

793. Dent, R. W. "Webster's Borrowings from Whetstone," *MLN,* 70 (1955): 568-570.

794. Izard, T. C. *George Whetstone, Mid-Elizabethan Gentleman of Letters.* Columbia University Studies in English and Comparative Literature, no. 158. New York, 1942.

795. Izard, T. C. "The Principal Source for Marlowe's *Tamburlaine,*" *MLN,* 58 (1943): 411-417.

796. Prouty, C. T. "George Whetstone and the Sources of *Measure for Measure,*" *SQ,* 15 (1964): 131-145.

797. Purcell, H. D. "Whetstone's *English Myrror* and Marlowe's *Jew of Malta,*" *N&Q,* 13 (1966): 288-290.

798. Stroup, T. B. *"Promos and Cassandra* and the *Law Against Lovers,*" *RES,* 8 (1932): 309-310.

WILLIAM SHAKESPEARE

Rape of Lucrece (1594)

799. Allen, D. C. "Some Observations on the *Rape of Lucrece,*" *ShS,* 15 (1962): 89-98.

800. Cummings, L. A. "The Purpose and Style of the *Rape of Lucrese,*" *ShN,* 3 (1953): 37.

801. Faber, M. D. *"Tess* and the *Rape of Lucrece,*" *ELN,* 5 (1968): 292-293.

802. Frye, R. M. "Shakespeare's Composition of *Lucrece:* New Evidence," *SQ,* 16 (1965): 289-296.

803. Hunter, G. K. "A Source for Shakespeare's *Lucrece?" N&Q,* 197 (1952): 46.

804. Hynes, S. "The Rape of Tarquin," *SQ,* 10 (1959): 451-453.

805. Kuhl, E. P. "Shakespeare's *Rape of Lucrece,*" *PQ,* 20 (1941): 352-360.

806. Marschall, W. "Das 'Argument' zu Shakespeare's *Lucrece,*" *Anglia,* 53 (1929): 102-122.

807. Marschall, W. "Das Troja-Gemälde in Shakespeare's *Lucrece,*" *Anglia,* 54 (1930): 83-96.

808. Montgomery, R. L., Jr. "Shakespeare's Gaudy: the Method of the *Rape of Lucrece*," in *Studies in Honor of DeWitt T. Starnes,* ed. by T. P. Harrison, A. A. Hill, E. C. Mossner, and J. Stedd. Austin, 1967, pp. 25-36.

809. Muir, K. "The *Rape of Lucrece,*" *Anglica,* 5 (1964): 25-40.

810. Starnes, D. T. "Geoffrey Fenton, Seneca and Shakespeare's *Lucrece,*" *PQ,* 43 (1964): 280-283.

811. Sylvester, B. "Natural Mutability and Human Responsibility: Form in Shakespeare's *Lucrece,*" *CE,* 26 (1965): 505-511.

812. Tolbert, J. M. "The Argument of Shakespeare's *Lucrece:* Its Sources and Authorship," *TSE,* 29 (1950): 77-90.

813. Tolbert, J. M. "A Source of Shakespeare's *Lucrece,*" *N&Q,* 198 (1953): 14-15.

814. Walley, H. R. "The *Rape of Lucrece* and Shakespearean Tragedy," *PMLA,* 76 (1961): 480-487.

815. Withington, R. " 'Vice' and 'Parasite'. A Note on the Evolution of the Elizabethan Villain," *PMLA,* 49 (1934): 743-751.

THOMAS KYD

Cornelia (1594)

816. McDiarmid, M. P. "A Reconsidered Parallel between Shakespeare's *King John* and Kyd's *Cornelia,*" *N&Q,* 3 (1956): 507-508.

IV. APPENDIX: WORKS IN NEED OF FURTHER SCHOLARSHIP

IV. APPENDIX: WORKS IN NEED OF FURTHER SCHOLARSHIP

IV. Appendix: Works in Need of Further Scholarship (complementing materials included under Sections I, II; see Farnham's 244, 699)

A. Non-dramatic Tragedy

JOHN SKELTON

Of the Death of the Noble Prince, Kynge Edwarde the Forth (included in the *Myrroure*)

FRANCIS DINGLEY

The Lamentation of King James IV (included in the *Myrroure*)

SIR DAVID LYNDSAY

The Tragedy of the Late Most Reuerende Father Dauid, by the Mercie of God Cardinall and Archbishoppe of Sainct Andrewes

[SIR NICHOLAS THROCKMORTON]

Throckmorton's Ghost

THOMAS CHURCHYARD

The Firste Parte of Chuchyardes Chippes (containing *Syr Symon Burleis Tragedy*)

A General Rehearsall of Warres or Churchyardes Choise (containing *A Heauie Matter of a Englishe Gentleman, and a Gentlewoman, in Maner of a Tragedie; A Pirates Tragedie*)

Churchyardes Challenge (containing *The Earle of Murtons Tragedie; A Tragicall Discourse of a Dolorous Gentlewoman*)

GEORGE FERRERS', JOHN HIGGINS', and THOMAS BLENNERHASSET'S contributions to editions of the *Myrroure*

RICHARD ROBINSON

The Rewarde of Wickednesse (collection)

ULPIAN FULWELL

The Flower of Fame (containing *The Lamentable Complaint of King James of Scotlande; The Lamentation of King James*)

GEORGE WHETSTONE

The Rocke of Regard (containing *The Disordered Life of Bianca Maria; Cressids Complaint*)

ANTHONY MUNDAY

The Mirrour of Mutabilitie

WILLIAM WYRLEY

The True Vse of Armorie (containing *The Glorious Life and Honorable Death of Sir Iohn Chandos; The Honorable Life and Languishing Death of Sir Iohn de Gralhy*)

ANTHONY CHUTE

> *Beawtie Dishonoured Written vnder the Title of Shores Wife*

THOMAS STORER

> *The Life and Death of Thomas Wolsey Cardinall*

B. Dramatic Tragedy

ANON.

> *Nice Wanton*

JANE LUMLEY

> *Iphigenia in Aulis*

ALEXANDER NEVILLE

> *Oedipus* (translation of Seneca)

THOMAS NUCE

> *Octavia* (translation of Seneca)

JOHN STUDLEY

> *Agamemnon* (translation of Seneca)
>
> *Hercules Oetaeus* (translation of Seneca)
>
> *Hippolytus* (translation of Seneca)
>
> *Medea* (translation of Seneca)

THOMAS GARTER

> *Most Virtuous and Godly Susanna*

WILLIAM GOLDINGHAM

> *Herodes*

THOMAS NEWTON

> *Thebais*

ANON.

> *Solymannidae*

ANON.

Timon

MARY HERBERT, COUNTESS OF PEMBROKE

Antonius (Antony)

ANON.

I, II *Troublesome Raigne of John, King of England*

ANON.

Famous Historye of the Life and Death of Captaine Thomas Stukeley

SAMUEL BRANDON

Virtuous Octavia

DRAYTON, HATHAWAY, MUNDAY, WILSON

I, II *Sir John Oldcastle*

ANON.

True Chronicle Historie of the Whole Life and Death of Thomas, Lord Cromwell

V. PRIMARY AND SECONDARY
AUTHOR INDEX

V. PRIMARY AND SECONDARY AUTHOR INDEX

PRIMARY AUTHORS

SECONDARY AUTHORS

COMPILERS

COMPILERS

David L. Middleton, assistant professor of English. Took B.A. degree at Jamestown College in North Dakota; M.A. at Purdue University; and Ph.D. at the University of Wisconsin, Madison, Wisconsin, in 1969. Joined staff of Trinity University in 1969 as specialist in the Renaissance and Shakespeare.

Associate Professor Harry B. Caldwell received the B.A. degree from Westminster College (Mo.), the M.A. and Ph.D. degrees from Vanderbilt University. His areas of special interest are the Medieval and Renaissance English and Scottish Ballads and the interpenetration of popular and literary tragic forms in the Middle Ages. He has taught at Trinity since 1968.